Special C

The Rise and Fall of a Cut Price Spy

CHRIS BOYD

Acknowledgements

I am indebted to my dear friend Brian Sperrin for his skilful kick starting of my ageing memory banks and for his confirmation of events that took place in South East Asia. To David Snell likewise for reminding me of escapades that took place and some of which we shared in the Far East. To Jim Hall for his confirmation of events in the Australian bush. To Laurie Bean for taking the trouble to look into and subsequently confirm details concerning a location in the NW of the Malay Peninsular. To my friend since our early days as teenagers in the RAF, John Jones, for his confirmation of events in the Hong Kong New Territories. To Brian Mudge and his fellow members of the 367 Signals Unit Association, for confirmation of some of the events I have written about that took place in the early 1950s in Hong Kong. To the RAF Habanniya Association for confirmation of other events. To Paul Beaumont for his encouragement and his reading of my draft. To Tony Nash for his encouragement and expert editing of my draft. Finally, to my dear niece Helen Markham and my very good friend, now sadly, the late Baz Barlett for prodding and encouraging me to sit down and write in the first place, without their encouragement this book would not have been written.

CONTENTS

INTRODUCTION

This sets out to tell of my recruitment into the world of electronic espionage, more commonly and correctly referred to as SIGINT (Signals Intelligence) early on in my Royal Air Force career and my subsequent employment in this field. It spans a period of some eighteen of my twenty-three years service journeying from the delights of Hong Kong to the intrigue of Berlin during the Cold War. To South East Asia during the period of the 'Undeclared War' between Indonesia and Malaysia 1963 - 1966, some of the time in remote locations and a two and a half year tour as a desk jockey with the Australian Defence Department in Melbourne.

Much of this time, although wearing the uniform of the RAF I was in effect, indirectly employed by GCHQ (Government Communications Headquarters) or its Australian counterpart DSD (Defence Signals Directorate). In the time I was located at DSD in Melbourne uniform was not worn. Both these organisations and their American opposite number NSA (National Security Agency) employ a large number of Civil or Public Servants. What is not generally realised however is, that throughout the world many thousands of cut-price spies from the Armed Forces of these countries are likewise engaged often seated alongside their civilian counterparts. Armed forces personnel so employed may be attending to these tasks in uncomfortable and at times dangerous situations on land, on the sea and in the air. Generally, in conditions that their civilian counterparts would not and would not even be expected to tolerate and are doing so for considerably less monetary rewards. I do realise of course that in recent years a number of GCHQ civilians have served in support of service personal in war zones such as Iraq and Afghanistan but these are exceptional circumstances. In normal situations the civilian operator, on the completion of his watch or his days work goes home to enjoy his free time doing whatever he wishes. Not so the armed forces operator who may have a number of so-called extraneous duties to perform in addition to his normal operational commitments. Not forgetting of

1

course the occasional parade to both prepare for and in which to take part. Even, in some cases that I have experience of, compulsory participation in sports or 'keep-fit' programmes. I am not complaining here, anyone joining the armed forces is aware of what is expected of him in addition to performing the duties involved in his chosen trade. It is merely an observation to highlight the difference between service and civilian personnel whilst doing the same job in the sigint world.

No book of this nature would be possible without the inclusion of some technical details of methods and equipment used. I have tried however, not to go too deeply into these details and hope I have succeeded. At the same time, I apologise to the technically knowledgeable reader if I have over simplified anything.

The reader may be forgiven for thinking that the age of operators sitting in front of a short-wave radio receiver, headphones clamped to head, listening to and taking down messages sent in Morse code are long gone. Indeed some articles in the media over the last decade or so would have given weight to such thoughts. Obviously, with the technological advances that have taken place in the last few decades such as the use of satellites and microwaves replacing most of the previous short-wave telecommunications systems the equipment in use is now more likely to be a computer screen than a radio receiver. However, if one listens on the short wave frequencies one can still hear, both Morse and Voice, illicit, diplomatic or military and naval transmissions in Morse code and a variety of languages, mostly I hasten to add, from what is referred to as the 'Eastern Bloc'. In addition to the European originated transmissions, some Chinese, Cuban diplomatic or illicit signals traffic is audible in Australia and the USA respectively and at times in the right atmospheric conditions, in the UK. With this in mind, there is still, no doubt, some dedicated operator tasked with continuing to intercept these signals but he/she will no longer be using the old-fashioned time honoured methods with a number of sharpened pencils at his/her elbow, using one to transcribe intercepted messages on to a pad. It is however, of these latter methods that this book is mainly concerned.

In order to show that it was not all work and no play much of what I have described relates to off-duty antics and time enjoyed with some of the best friends and colleagues that one could possibly wish to have. Also covered is my being, albeit over a beer or two, in the company of one of the 20th Centuries most infamous and successful Soviet Spies and later having the misfortune to have another of the same ilk as a colleague.

Some of the locations in which my colleagues and I found ourselves were, during WWII the scenes of much bloodshed and infamy. During our time in such places, whilst we had a scant knowledge of the recent history of these regions we really knew very little. With the advent of the internet so many people, like myself have become more enlightened and I have therefore, in some cases included a few historical notes for the readers' interest.

During my career in Signals Intelligence I would never have considered or even thought of referring to work of this nature as spying. It would seem however, that gathering intelligence in this way is now looked upon by the media as just another form of eavesdropping and therefore a form of spying. GCHQ is rarely mentioned in the press without the word spy or spying being included in the report or article that one reads. Likewise during my seven years spent in Cyprus in retirement there was one prolific anti-British writer to the press who continually referred to the British Spy bases on the island. He was of course referring to British sigint bases there. In the light of such revelations and references appearing in the public domain I am led to follow the lead, hence my choice of sub-title for this book that I hope dear reader you will enjoy.

1 THE 'MET' SCHEME

Having joined the Royal Air Force as a 16-year-old Boy Entrant and upon completion of my training as a Telegraphist I was, in December 1949 initially posted to the United Kingdom's RAF Main Signals Centre at Stanbridge, close to the town of Leighton Buzzard in Bedfordshire. Here I was employed on all the routine telecommunications duties for which I had been trained. Indeed, in my first few months at Stanbridge I was to have hands-on experience in almost all the tasks expected of a trained Telegraphist except using the Aldis signalling lamp and in RDF (Radio Direction Finding). The lamp I was never to use operationally but was to have the chance to put my knowledge of RDF to good use during my first overseas tour. Whilst undergoing my eighteen months training at Compton Bassett in Wiltshire, I enjoyed much of the course and the RDF training sessions were a particular favourite. One or sometimes two trainees would laboriously cycle around the camp roads on a tricycle that had a large box attached to its front rather like the ice-cream man that was a common site in the UK in days gone by. All this tricycle needed to give it an authentic appearance was a sign emblazoned with the words, 'Stop Me and Buy One'. The box in this case did not, unfortunately, contain such confection but held a radio transmitter or signal generator with a Morse key and a retractable antenna on its upper surface. Using the Morse key the cyclist, when stationary of course, would put out a call requesting a bearing using abbreviations from the International or ICAO (International Civil Aviation Organisation) 'Q' code, for example, 'INT QTE.' INT being the interrogative or question indicator and QDM meaning 'what is my true bearing from your station'? To give some variety to the exercise he would also use other Q signals such as one to request a course to steer. This transmission would, hopefully, be received by his classmates sitting in a HFDF (High Frequency Direction Finding) cabin/classroom elsewhere within the school complex. These trainees would, when receiving the request for a bearing, use a radio goniometer to take such a bearing and they would then plot the cyclists' position on a map. Not that the cyclist would act on this bearing when it was transmitted back to him, he would simply toddle off to another location and repeat the exercise. Such simple training methods may these days appear somewhat Heath-Robinson and even laughable but they were effective.

After about eighteen months at Stanbridge, I was summoned, with a small number of others to report to RAF Station Hednesford on Cannock Chase in Staffordshire where we were to be interviewed by Wing Commander Swanborough RAF Retired, no other details were forthcoming. Hednesford was at that time a recruit training centre, and also for a short period of time before it moved to Lytham St Anne's in 1951, a PDU (Personnel Despatch Unit) where airmen were usually accommodated whilst awaiting conveyance by sea or air (mostly sea in those days) to their overseas destinations. As we were not recruits nor were we expecting an overseas posting it was a puzzled party of airmen that arrived at Hednesford. On arrival there we were instructed to report to a wooden hut, of which there were many, all identical and of the type of building in which about 18 - 20 airmen would normally be billeted. The hut to which we were directed was, apart from the usual rows of, to put it into service jargon, beds iron, airmen for the use of, quite empty. However, the small room at the end of the hut where normally the Corporal in charge of this particular hut would reside was not empty but was occupied by two gentlemen in civilian clothes, one of them, the one who introduced himself, did all the talking and asked all the questions was the aforementioned retired Wing Commander. The other chap, presumably his assistant did not have much to say but just seemed to be taking everything in and making notes. We were all interviewed individually and during the course of the interview we were asked if we would like to join what was, at that time, referred to as the 'Met' Scheme, a title that most suspected had nothing to do with the weather but was shrouded in mystery. With this mysterious carrot dangling before me I eagerly accepted the offer and found that I was about to be enrolled not into any 'Met' scheme which in reality did not exist but into the 'Y' service.

The Y service was initially formed in WWI, and continued to operate extensively in WWII its purpose being to intercept enemy radio traffic. The organisation was manned by both male and female operators from all three armed services and a number of civilian organisations. Some amateur radio enthusiasts were also co-opted to perform radio intercept duties in their own homes. The activities of the Y service did not cease at the end of the war; however, the onset of the cold war in Europe was to reveal that it was still very necessary and indeed opportune to continue to gather intelligence via the ether on the movements and intentions of any potential enemies. Sigint was also to prove its worth in a number of the so-called 'small wars' from the Korean conflict in the early 1950s, the Cypriot EOKA liberation conflict 1955 -1959 and further Greek/Turkish problems in 1963 through to the Indonesian Confrontation 1963 - 1966 and in the Falklands campaign in 1982.

In addition to the number of radio intercept or Y stations in the UK and beyond there are a number of active mobile platforms, on the ground, at sea and in the air that continue to be operational albeit with a reduced number of the static intercept stations. The introduction of satellites into the game together with other new technology has enabled such closures to take place, at the same time the remaining stations will have increased in size and no doubt expanded their area of operations. One main intercept site in the UK in this category, located at what was previously known as RAF Station Digby in Lincolnshire was no doubt able to absorb some of the tasks and personnel from the closures. As well as undergoing a name change to Joint Service Signals Unit (JSSU) it also found itself no longer exclusively RAF manned. The sigint unit there, was until a few short years ago, apart from having a civilian Met Officer, entirely RAF manned but has now become Tri-service, plus civilian with an added flavouring of US armed forces personnel. The Army and RAF however, are the majority incumbents. JSSU (D) (D for Digby). Digby is part of a larger network of Joint Signals

Units but is the largest of its kind. This station will frequently be referred to in some of the following chapters using the name I knew it by during my time in the Y service, RAF Digby.

Before those lucky lads that had been interviewed at RAF Hednesford and were subsequently selected for service in the Y scheme could be posted to one or other active intercept station they would have to undergo specialist radio operator training. The sixteen week training course at Cheadle in Staffordshire (not to be confused with Cheadle Cheshire which is now part of Greater Manchester) involved learning, in addition to the characters and symbols contained in the International Morse code in which they were already proficient and had experience in the use of, a number of extra characters that they had previously had no reason to be aware of. These extra characters would include the Cyrillic ones used in Russian and some other Eastern Bloc countries, all the European accented letters such as the French é and á, the German umlauts, the Spanish tilde and those odd Scandinavian ones. In addition, as Chinese Morse consisted of figures only but in an abbreviated form, these shortened figures also had to be learnt. Most of the Cyrillic characters when transmitted in Morse do not equate to an English character on the page. As an example a V (dit dit dit dah) in the international Morse code would equate to the symbol Ж in Russian. The intercepting operator would not of course be expected to write this character down in this form, if he was to try with any attempt at legibility then he would never be able to keep up with the message being transmitted at speed. He would write down the symbol as he heard it, the V. The analyst transcribing the end product would be the one to transcribe the message into its original form or simply translate same into English. So for the majority of an intercept containing Cyrillic characters the operator's job would be straight forward, he would simply write down what he was hearing. So why bother learning any extra elements one may ask. The answer is that the Russian alphabet contains a number of characters that have no symbol in the International Morse code. One of these, Ш is sent in Morse as dah dah dah dah and would be transcribed by the intercepting operator as H but with a line or dash above it. Another is I0 sent as dit dit dah dah and would be transcribed as U, again with a line or dash above it. These symbols written with the line above them are known to sigint operators as 'barred' letters. Again, the person analysing the end product would be aware of the meaning of such odd characters appearing on an operators log or message pad.

Not all the time in the classroom was spent wearing headphones, procedures necessary for the correct completion of ones logs and message forms had to be learned as did details of the call-sign systems and operational procedures of certain foreign countries. All countries being aware that their wireless communications are capable of being intercepted will institute measures to prevent this. One thing many will do, in addition to changing their operating frequencies, often on a daily basis, is to change their call signs. Therefore the ways and methods to counteract this and quickly find both the new frequencies in use and ascertain that the new call sign being heard relates to the one used on the previous day had to be learnt and digested.

Part way through the course the students or trainees as the RAF preferred to refer to them, were summoned to a large country manor house located a short walk .across the fields adjacent to the camp and close to the hamlet of Hammersley Hays. This fine house, known to some, as it still is to this day, as Woodhead Hall was during WWII, one of the principal 'Y' stations in the UK involved in intercepting mainly Morse code traffic of the Long-Range German Air Force and feeding it to Bletchley Park. Following the end of the war it continued to operate in its sigint role monitoring and analysing Soviet military communications traffic until its closure in 1995 when, at a later date, it was sold into private ownership.

It was here; in this manor house seated in a large comfortable office we were, once again to meet the same gentleman that had interviewed us at Hednesford, Wing Commander W.G. Swanborough RAF Retired. This fellow had been responsible for setting up the sigint station at RAF Cheadle in 1937 and remained the Commanding Officer of RAF Cheadle Y station throughout WWII. Following the end of the war all existing civilian sigint stations were being run by their respective Ministries, The Admiralty, The War Office and The Air Ministry. This situation remained until 1964 when they were all taken over by GCHQ and Wing Commander Swanborough, by then an Air Ministry civilian employee, became the first GCHQ civilian officer in charge of the Cheadle intercept station. [1] He was to retire shortly afterwards having served a record of 37 years in charge of a station. On his desk during my visit with others in 1951were a number of different coloured telephones, certainly one red and one green, the others were black and presumably the ones used for normal non-classified communications. The walls of this office were adorned with a number of large plastic or pottery ears adding to the atmosphere of secrecy and intrigue reminding one of the wartime slogan, 'Walls have Ears'. After a few initial questions such as "how are you enjoying the course" the main point of the interview was reached, "Where would you like to go following successful completion of the course", Germany or Hong Kong?. Habbaniya, fifty-five miles north of Baghdad in Iraq was also available but not offered to this particular class. Marvellous, I thought, being asked to where one would like to be posted, was this the Air Force in which I had voluntarily enlisted. Usually one went wherever someone sticking pins in a map back at the RAF Records Office in Gloucester wanted to send one. I think the more adventurous or those among us including myself, keen to see the world, chose Hong Kong. Those who maybe had girl friends or other 'ties' in their home town and possibly thought Germany would be nice, being able to pop home for Christmas etc, took the European option.

The strange thing is, I can remember a number of chaps in that same class and the ones that chose the Far East I often came across later in my career but the other European bound ones I never saw or heard of again. On receiving our replies and making notes the genial retired Wing Commander picked up one of the coloured telephones and speaking to the person at the other end of the line relayed our names and choice of posting. That was it, job done and a happy bunch of lads made their way back across the fields to don a pair of headphones and take down even more pre-recorded (on an old fashioned wire recorder) foreign Morse code for practice and to obtain the necessary qualifications to ensure successful completion of the course. Many years later, as a civilian and employed by a large pharmaceutical company, one of a team of girls in the order office asked me if I had ever met a Wing Commander Swanborough during my time in the RAF. Apparently she was related, not sure after all these years but I think he was her uncle, as the saying goes, 'small world'.

The only foreign language that most of us trainees initially found any difficulty writing and keeping up with in the Morse transmissions when sent at fast speeds was German. The reason for this being that the German word *die* (English the) has only one dash or dah followed by five dots or dits. Also there seems to be more words with the ie combination in German than any other language. But, as the saying goes practice makes perfect and we all found a way to write *die* and the other ie combinations at speed. The course was not, by any means easy and required a lot of concentration if one wanted to achieve the high standard required.

The lunch break of one hour soon came around and after a quick meal in the airmen's mess just about everyone headed for the NAAFI [2] for some relaxation and entertainment. We were fortunate in that a fellow trainee, a tall Liverpool lad who was an excellent pianist would entertain us for whatever time we had remaining before returning to the classroom. On one occasion my pal and I did not exit the NAAFI quickly enough for the liking of the little weasel admin corporal, I think we were making a phone call at the time and didn't respond to this fellow's screamed orders. Subsequently we were charged with failing to obey a lawful order and were sentenced to five days Confined to Camp or Jankers[3] as this form of punishment was referred to throughout Britain's armed forces. Unfortunately, this spell of jankers covered the week-end which meant that we were confined to camp on the Saturday when our fellow trainees were out enjoying themselves. The temptation to 'break camp' and nip down to the pub as soon as our last inspection at the guard room had been completed, which I think was at 2100 hours, overcame any thought of caution. So, a quick change into 'civvies' and head down into the town. Not that we were able to exit the camp via the main gate, this would have meant having to pass by the guard room. Not for us 'escapees' oh no, there was a gap in the fence that led to the airmen's married quarters that were located just outside camp. I think this gap must have been deliberately made by some of the instructors who lived with their families in these quarters and did not fancy the long walk home involved should they have taken the legitimate route via the main gate. Arriving at the pub and deciding to take our drinks into the back room found us in the company of two of our corporal instructors who, although surprised to see two of their trainees that they knew should not have been there, invited us to sit with them and have a chat as fellow tradesmen. In later years I was to meet up and serve with both these chaps, Bill Cody and Ginge Guerin on more than one posting and we became good friends. Unfortunately our evenings enjoyment in the pub was short-lived, who should walk in and give us an even bigger surprise but the 'weasel'. Nothing happened there and then but the Monday morning saw us once again up on a charge in front of the Commanding Officer being sentenced to a further and longer spell of jankers. Following our sentencing and about to head back to the classroom we were halted by a shout from the Station Adjutant, a Flight Lieutenant, who came out of the building behind us. He gave us a friendly talk which in essence was 'you two are doing so well on the course, let's not have any more stupidity'. Lesson learned, we took his advice, did not get into any further bother and indeed did do very well on the course.

Being unfortunate enough to be struck with a bad attack of toothache whilst at Cheadle put me off dentists for much of the remainder of my service. We had no resident dentist on the camp but one would visit from time to time and, as it happened he was due at about the same time that I had a need of his talents, otherwise I would probably have been sent to the nearest hospital that had a dental facility as was normally the case. This visiting dentist arrived in a 3-Ton Bedford truck, his surgery, having journeyed from a larger RAF Station some distance away but still in Staffordshire. One simply climbed into the back of the truck, sat in a chair and was given the necessary injection to freeze the gums. As the freeze procedure took about ten minutes I was told to go and sit in the passenger seat in the front of the truck and wait. Returning to the rear of the vehicle the offending back tooth was painfully extracted. I swore I would never go to a service dentist again, but I did many years later in Singapore when detachments to Borneo were on the agenda. There were, apparently, head-hunters in Borneo so plenty of opportunity to have ones head removed as I believe, many Japanese invaders found out some years previous but there was no one available to remove teeth so a visit to the dentist in Singapore was obligatory. I must however, afford the truck-borne dentist due credit for his skill. Apart from extracting the tooth that had been giving me problems he noticed a small break in the face of one of my front teeth, visible whenever I opened my mouth or smiled. Being the professional that he obviously was he attended to it there and then with a small, barely visible, filling Sixty three years on that filling remains in place, albeit slightly discoloured but I can hardly blame him for that, especially with all the red wine I have been bathing it in during the past few years.

Before setting sail to sample the delights of the Far East and to be introduced to the tasks that we had been trained for, perhaps a few words regarding the joys to be experienced in the small town of Cheadle are in order. One of the first things that new arrivals were to learn was that there were more single girls, or women in and around that particular town than men. Whoopee! was always the initial reaction and the lads, well most of them, waited with much youthful eagerness for Saturday to come around so that they could trip the light fantastic at the local 'hop' and maybe get lucky. It was certainly true that there were always plenty of partners to choose from at this event. I know of one lad who, when partnered with a girl that had to catch a bus home before the dance ended would escort his young lady to the bus then head smartly back to the dance to take up with another. A number of young men did marry girls from the town after what must have been a whirlwind romance. Two of the marriages did, to my knowledge, last and possibly there were more. My own girl friend there was also one who had to board a bus prior to the end of the dance. We took our time to say goodnight down a quiet alleyway prior to the arrival of the bus and I was happy just to return to my bed in the camp without any further assignations that evening. There was nothing permanent about the relationship and I did hear later that this young lady had married a local farmer's boy.

Most of us would spend the weekends in Cheadle, mainly to attend this joyful Saturday night event. Some weekends however a number of us would decide to get away home or visit somewhere else. One such Saturday around midday when trying to book a taxi to the railway station in Stoke-upon-Trent we were told that all the taxis were out at a wedding and all that was available was a hearse! Not wanting to forfeit any more of our precious weekend than was absolutely necessary we said, "Send it". They did and whilst two or three of the party were able to sit up front, the remainder of us piled in the back raising more than a few eyebrows en-route to the station.

Cheadle was one of the two most relaxed and bullshit free stations that I ever had the pleasure to serve on, the other we come on to later. We were though, from time-to-time, reminded that we were indeed still in the real Royal Air Force by the appearance of the very large and imposing figure of the SWO (Station Warrant Officer) the RAFs equivalent of the British Army's Regimental Sergeant Major. Warrant Officer Marsh, known to all and sundry as 'Swampy', was rarely to be seen when not being followed around by his faithful Boxer dog, Chunky. When asked why the name Chunky for a dog, he is known to have replied, "Because he has square testicles". I believe that Cheadle, because of its small size qualified for nothing higher than a Squadron Leader or at the most a Wing Commander as its station commander. Consequently it would not have been rated as a station necessitating a

Warrant Officer SWO; in such instances a Flight Sergeant would have filled this post. Swampy was no longer a young man, and as long-serving personnel were often granted their choice of final posting. One normally would choose a station close to home or where they may have wished to retire, perhaps this was Swampy's choice and an exception was made in this case. I do believe that Swampy was himself also very happy to be serving at this small relaxed station because he never seemed to give anyone any real aggravation, that was left to his little Corporal, the Weasel. Swampy had I suppose, to justify his existence there and that took the form of insisting that our barrack rooms were always very clean and tidy with the bed packs properly in place at all times other than when were sleeping. His only concession to bullshit was his insistence on us having our webbing packs on display with the brass fittings looking nice and shiny. He would always seem to be in evidence on Wednesday afternoons that in the RAF is traditionally 'Sports Afternoon'. I don't recall much in the way of sport taking place there apart from just about everyone going on a long cross-country run. I am sure Swampy made his presence felt at this time to ensure that everyone did indeed go on this run and that no one skived off. During one of these runs when my pal and I were first home and taking a bath, (I don't recall there being any showers) who should appear but Swampy, he either did not believe that we had been on the run or that we had shortened the course to our liking so he detailed us off to the cookhouse kitchen to perform a few menial tasks. He later appeared in the kitchen accompanied by Chunky so my pal and I took the opportunity to determine if deformed testicles were the real reason for this friendly creature being named this way. I have to report that we were not able to confirm this one way or the other. I must say that Swampy was never nasty or over officious in his dealings with his flock, I don't think he had a nasty bone in his body and I do hope that he and Chunky had a long and happy retirement together.

Another pleasant aspect to Cheadle was that there were no parades, of any sort. Parades I can understand when they are necessary for some or other ceremonial but at many stations they often featured for no apparent reason apart from making the personage taking the salute or barking the orders feel important. Anyway, we simply did not have a barrack square or any other similar area suitable to hold a parade upon. The nearest we ever came to such was the time when we were all lined up on the roadway in our best 'blues' to be inspected and selected for duty as pall bearers, escorts and firing party at a military funeral. The deceased was not one of our number but an unfortunate airman who was stationed elsewhere and whose home was in a nearby town. Spending a period of leave at home he suffered a fatal accident in the local swimming pool and his family requested, as was their right, a military funeral. It fell to Cheadle as his nearest RAF base to provide the necessary personnel for the ceremony that took place in the nearby town of Newcastle-under-Lyme.

I no longer remember if there was any celebration on completion of the course at Cheadle but I am sure some of us must have had a few drinks together before heading off in different directions to our respective homes to enjoy a week or so of embarkation leave. Our instructions were to report to 5 PDU at RAF Hednesford on a given date in August 1951. This was however, not to happen as whilst at home we each were to receive a telegram extending our leave and informing us that 5 PDU was in the progress of moving further north to Lytham St. Anne's near Blackpool, just 50 miles away from my home. As the date we were to report gave me more time at home I decided that, having always been compelled to display a 'short back and sides' head of hair, I would encourage my sideboards to take on a new length, not a good idea as it turned out.

Reporting to Lytham on the given date and meeting up with my pals again it was not long before I was spotted by the SWO who almost had an apoplectic fit on spotting my facial growth of which I had become rather proud. Fortunately for me this re-located PDU was in such chaos that the SWO had his hands full with much more important matters and I escaped with nothing more than a severe bollocking and being ordered to remove the sideboards without delay. Should the PDU have not been in the state it was he would certainly have taken my name and possibly detailed me off to perform some menial job of work as a punishment. The place was indeed in a mess, the Nissan huts in which we were to be billeted were mostly without windows. They had all of course had windows at some time but what few remained were broken, no doubt by vandals or young lads wandering around prior to the camp being re-opened. The catering staff was certainly having a hard time because, it seemed errors had been made in the estimation of supplies required to feed a large number of hungry mouths. One WAAF catering officer was running around like a headless chicken trying to get things organised and at the same time informing everyone that they were rationed to two slices of bread with their evening meal.

Being by now mid-summer a few of us took advantage of this prime holiday location and ventured into Blackpool to enjoy a few drinks in some of the many hotel bars. The same few even had a dip in the sea in their underpants alongside the central pier. This being to the amusement of a number of young girls on the pier above. Such joys were soon to come to an end and all the Far East bound lads were bussed off to Liverpool to board the good ship Lancashire, or to give it its official title, His Majesty's Transport (HMT) Lancashire, a ship under the Bibby Line flag. She was crewed mainly by Lascars; apart from the officers and a number of other seamen such as the cooks and bakers that is.

Leaving Britain's shores for the first time in my young life one fine August evening I was soon to experience the effects of a stormy passage through the Bay of Biscay. I almost began to wonder what, after all, I had let myself in for. Happily, this short but unpleasant episode was soon behind me and standing on the deck of HMT Lancashire I gazed in wonder at hundreds of tiny white houses bathed in bright sunshine and covering the distant shoreline of what I assumed to be Portugal. Here I was starting to see, albeit at a distance, lands that I had so far only heard of or seen in my school atlas.

Having digested my first view of a foreign land I was more than pleased to be on deck again when we dropped anchor a little way off shore in Gibraltar. There was the famous 'Rock' also bathed in bright Mediterranean sunshine. I was beginning to think that it was only Manchester, place of my birth that had cloudy skies. A lot of activity was taking place around the ship including the disembarkation of a passenger who had fallen ill and was being taken ashore by an RAF tender. I immediately became fascinated by this place and promised myself that, one day, I would return to visit and stay a while. This I was not to do until the late 1980s, I was not disappointed. On the next leg of the journey the waters were somewhat calmer and I enjoyed with fascination the sight of Dolphins keeping up with the ship and obviously enjoying speeding along in its bow waves. The memory of the sight of these beautiful creatures will remain with me forever.

Our next port-of-call was Port Said at the mouth of the Suez Canal. I must admit that although I found the experience of being anchored here for a short while very interesting it is not a place to which I have had any yearning to return. The ship was surrounded by small craft known as 'Bum Boats' from which the occupants were offering a proliferation of souvenirs for sale. As these small boats were in the water a good distance below the side of the ship the purchases had to hauled aboard in a small basket attached to a long thin rope and the payment made in the reverse direction. The rope initially being thrown up to the ship by the vendors and then tied to the deck rail. I was starting to wonder what would happen if one took the goods but failed to pay up. I did not have to wonder for long, one soldier chancing his arm, did just that, took delivery of the goods but failed to send the cash. A big mistake, the Arab vendor was quickly on board and in pursuit; how he managed this from so far below the side of the ship I have no idea. I did not view the outcome but as there were no reports of a soldier having his throat cut I assumed he had either paid up or successfully evaded confrontation with the vendor. We were allowed ashore for a short time whilst the ship took on water and whatever else it needed. Here I was to see for the first time, what is now commonplace in many parts of Europe, an Arab female wearing a

Burqa. I was also to realise that all those tales of natives selling *'Feelthy post-cards'* to the troops were not fiction; my colleagues and I were continually pestered in the dock area to purchase such cards. In the streets we were also approached and assailed with the whispered word, *Exhibition.* An invite to what was obviously not a display of fine art but a pornographic show of sorts. Following previous advice we didn't accept any such invitations. For me one word sums up Port Said, *Sleaze.* An experience never to be forgotten but we were glad to get back on board and continue on our way further east.

The journey through the Suez Canal was, in parts interesting enough but not particularly exciting. Mid-way we were to pass by the British Forces HQ at Ismaïlia on the west bank where there was a large RAF contingent manning the Middle East Signals Centre. I remember thanking my lucky stars at the time that I had accepted the offer to join the 'Y' service and had, in consequence, avoided what was deemed to be a most unpopular posting. We did at least once come upon a lone Arab taking a dip in the canal. When we were alongside he would quickly flip on to his back and 'flash'. Mucky sod, his aquatic gyrations were, I assume, aimed at the ladies who were looking over the ships rail at the time. There were a number of female passengers on board, not service personnel but wives en-route to join their servicemen husbands stationed in the Far East. There was at least one female UK Civil Servant among the passengers that I enjoyed a dance with at one of the organised functions.

Once through the canal and the Red Sea we arrived at the port of Aden. Aden was until 1963 a British Crown Colony and in November 1967 became The Peoples Republic of South Yemen marking the end of British Rule there. The first thing everyone realised upon arrival in the port was that it was hot, really hot. I remember we had to queue on board in the heat to be inspected and have our names ticked off on a list before going ashore. One lad in line, obviously an educated type insisted on informing all and sundry that Aden was known as 'The White Man's Grave'. Such a gem of information we could have done without whilst standing there feeling the sweat running down our backs. We could well have done without the inspection also as, within a very short time our khaki drill uniforms would, in part, appear as though they had just come out of the washing machine. The area we were put ashore was known as Steamer Point, I don't remember there being much of interest there except a number of bars and a few shops selling duty free goods, which we could not afford. Naturally enough it was not long before we ventured into one of the bars, one in which, to this day, I cannot account for my strange behaviour. My four companions at this time gasping for something to quench their thirst ordered a beer, I'll never forget, it was Stella, a fine Belgian brew. Me, I ordered a coke or something similar. No amount of persuasion or Mickey taking by the others made me change my mind. I have never been able to explain this to myself particularly as I enjoyed a beer and on board the ship we were rationed to one small can per person per day.

The journey onward to Ceylon (Sri Lanka) was, as I remember calm seas all the way. Docking in the port of Colombo, the countries capital, in fine sunshine I quickly noticed the absence of the oppressive heat we had experienced in Aden. Here we were also allowed ashore for a few hours. It was not long before we were assailed by rickshaw owners wanting to take us to a place of entertainment, an *exhibition.* Obviously the same 'treat' that we had been offered in Port Said. Again our small party resisted such delights and we did our own bit of sightseeing. At one stage we came upon a large official looking sea front building, probably the town hall or something similar. One of our number, 'Spud' Murray a lad from Middlesbrough looking at said building exclaimed "Ah, perhaps that is where the exhibition is". This stopped the rest of us in our tracks and we all gaped at Spud thinking he was joking. He wasn't, poor innocent Spud, he really had thought those sleazy types had been offering us some sort of cultural experience. He had a lot to learn. How he became known as Spud I have no idea, many readers will know that such a nickname is usually bestowed upon those with the name Murphy not Murray. Sightseeing over it was time to head back to the docks and board our transport once again. The RAF contingent or Draft as it was referred to were not the only passengers on this vessel. In fact, the majority were soldiers from various Regiments and Corps of the British Army, most bound for Korea where a fierce and bloody battle in incredible conditions was raging. I do wonder sometimes how many of those soldiers, our sea-borne companions, failed to return. A number of them, particularly from one of the famous Scottish Regiments got up to a number of daring antics on board. Such antics included swinging by rope from one upper deck to an open one below. This meant that for a few brief seconds their body would be out over the open sea. Foolhardy maybe but brave, and they seemed to enjoy it immensely. I like to think that this sort of adventurous and daring spirit was to serve them well in battle in Korea.

Singapore was arrived at after a relatively short and uneventful onward journey. As this was as far as HMT Lancashire was going we disembarked and were taken to RAF Changi in a number of 3-Ton trucks. Here, those of us destined to continue eastwards spent a lazy couple of weeks in transit accommodation that consisted of large and airy barrack blocks that had everything we needed. Enough showers for everyone to indulge after the not-so-good salt water showers on the troopship and sufficient ceiling fans to keep the warm air circulating. Much of the time was enjoyed swimming in the Pagar, a section of the sea cordoned off by a shark-proof (we hoped) fence. When not getting wet in the Pagar or getting sunburnt elsewhere we would retire to the station's Malcolm Club to enjoy a cool refreshing drink, usually tea, coffee or a soft drink. Little did I think at that time that I would in a few years time spend four enjoyable and exciting years in this delightful location. Being awakened early one morning by the shouts of a native orderly we were instructed to pack our kit and await transport to the docks to board a ship bound for Hong Kong.

HMT Empire Halladale, once a German cruise liner named the *Antonio Delfino* had at one time, in Hitler's Germany, been used as a *Kraft durch Freude* (Strength though Joy) pleasure vessel to send selected Aryan boys and girls of the Hitler Youth organisations off on a pleasure cruise to South America. The object being that many of the young ladies would return in the condition that would help to ensure the perpetuation of the 'Master Race'. At the end of WWII this vessel was taken in prize by the Royal Navy and from August 1946 to August 1947 was used on Government Service between Tilbury and Cuxhaven. From 1947 she was used as a troopship managed by the Anchor Line, Glasgow and in February 1948 evacuated the last British troops (the Black Watch) from India. Sad to have to relate, my experience of this vessel in 1951 was anything but pleasurable. The food on the Lancashire, of which I had no complaints, was served to us on those metal compartmentalised trays in a civil, indeed courteous manner by the Lascar kitchen staff. On the Halladale the food both unappetising and almost inedible was slopped or thrown on to the same metal trays by a sweaty, overweight bare-chested member of the kitchen crew, made up of my fellow countrymen. This particular fellow was obviously not happy in his work. The only saving grace on this vessel, its home port being Glasgow, was the daily issue of one can of McEwen's beer. Not that this particular brand was any better than some others but the can it was served in featured pictures of attractive scantily clad young ladies. A pleasant diversion for most of the lads. One 'ceremony' on board both vessels that always amused the RAF Draft was the Captains inspection that was carried out on a number of days throughout the voyage. Luckily we all slept in 'standees', these were fold down metal beds in the form of 3-tier bunks as opposed to hammocks that were the norm on some of the other troopships. During the inspection these beds had to be folded down into the sleeping positions and all the service passengers had to lie on them. As the Captain and his entourage, the inspecting party, arrived on the deck to be inspected the person whom I took to be the Sergeant Major would shout, in a strident manner, "Lie to attention". This really did amuse us RAF types, I suppose the army were used to such nonsense. The first time it happened, as one could only expect, much sniggering could be heard throughout the deck. This was soon silenced by another louder and angry shout from the Sergeant Major.

Following a journey of which I think took little more than one week we were all pleased to arrive in Hong Kong to settle in to a working routine and start to earn our keep.

2 JOYS OF THE ORIENT

There were, and indeed still are, a number of British or British Commonwealth Signals Intelligence gathering stations throughout the world, some operated solely by civilian 'spies', others jointly by service and civilian personnel and some entirely by armed forces operators. One such station that was initially manned exclusively by armed forces personnel but later Australianised and civilianised, now no longer in existence since the Chinese took back Hong Kong in 1997 was No.367 Signals Unit, Royal Air Force Station Little Sai Wan. This station was sited in a bay on the north side of Hong Kong Island with the living accommodation located at Cape Collinson some two miles further east along the coast. Some airmen were billeted in Nissan huts and others in the 'caves' which were little more than dugouts carved into the rock face of the hillside. It soon became obvious that this accommodation would not be satisfactory forever as the caves tended to be very damp, the Nissan huts cramped and although a number of new ones were being erected, many were well past their sell by date.

The obvious solution to the accommodation problem, eventually arrived at, was to billet everyone close to their place of work on the operational site. To this end, in 1952, work began on the building of a number of new barrack blocks and supporting buildings such as a cookhouse and its adjacent dining facility in addition to similar buildings to accommodate and care for the Officers and senior ranks. While this was taking place everyone was moved to temporary accommodation in Lye Mun Barracks, where elements of the British army and units of the Royal Hong Kong Defence Force were also accommodated. At one stage there I was to witness what must have been hundreds of young Chinese Males gathered around the tightly closed main gate. It was on this particular day that recruiting was taking place for the volunteer force and this gathering represented the hopefuls. As only a very limited number were required on such occasions the majority of those gathered at the gate who were all to rush in when it was opened, would be disappointed. I'm sure that the really determined ones would keep on trying to 'join up' until they became either too old or infirm to be accepted.

Lye Mun Barracks was situated close to Shau Kei Wan one of the main populated areas of the island in the district of Chai Wan. In 1941 this was the scene of fierce fighting in defence of the island by Canadian troops who were to suffer a large number of casualties.[4] The Canadians as well as local troops together with British and Indian units were hopelessly outnumbered by the Japanese. Not all those killed died on the battlefield however, many were bayoneted to death by the Japanese along with their nurses whilst lying wounded in their beds in a makeshift hospital. [5]

The only relics of war remaining there when we were moved from Cape Collinson were a number of concrete Pill Boxes still dotted around the area sloping down towards the small beach at Lye Mun Gap. Together with one of my colleagues I sometimes visited these relics but little of interest remained. There were also a large number of caves dug into the hillside that we also spent some time investigating and did often wonder who had actually done the digging. Was it the allies or the Japanese? We never did find out and there was nothing in there to give us any indication. Should such things as the metal detectors that are on the market today have been available at that time perhaps both the Pill Boxes and the caves may have produced some interesting, but possibly explosive, finds. As Lye Mun Gap is the eastern gateway into Hong Kong harbour we always had a bird's eye view of all the shipping entering and leaving the harbour and many a pleasant hour was spent on the hillside or on the roof of a barrack block ship spotting. Some of the larger British and US Naval vessels were a rewarding sight as they made their way slowly through the gap. One Royal Navy Frigate that could sometimes be seen was HMS Amethyst [6] of the famed Yangtze Incident. On 20 April 1949, HMS Amethyst was on her way from Shanghai to Nanking when she was fired upon by the Chinese People's Liberation Army and remained trapped in China until 30 July 1949 before making a spectacular escape [7] that was dramatised in the 1957 film *Yangtze*

Incident. HMS Amethyst returned to the UK for a refit in 1950 but was re-commissioned and returned to the Far East where she remained until 1952. Had the Amethyst not returned to Hong Kong from the UK then we would not have had the privilege to see a vessel that featured in a most heroic, and eventual triumphant incident. A peace-time event that was sadly to result in considerable loss of life and serious injury being occasioned by the brave crews of this and three other ships involved.

Moving into Lye Mun's large and airy purpose-built barrack blocks from cramped Nissan huts or caves was appreciated by most until they came to bed down for the first time. Many of the rooms in these large blocks had not been used for some time and their total furnishings were 'Beds Iron,' or Iron bedsteads. Any bedding except the mattress to go with the beds had to be obtained from the bedding store as was normal practice wherever one ended up. Standard issue was usually a couple of sheets and blankets, a pillow and three biscuits that are not edible but are three square-shaped flock filled objects that when placed on the bed in line made a mattress. Normally these Biscuits would already be in place on the beds but we were soon to realise the reason why this was not so in this case. Whilst the rooms were not inhabited, the beds were, by vicious biting bed-bugs. Following a sleepless night by many, war was declared on the bugs. The first move was to speak with the Army residents of an adjacent block who showed no surprise when a couple of sleepy airmen showed up asking questions. Their only advice to remove the pests that they had at some time also experienced was, 'burn the buggers'. Setting fire to the biscuits didn't seem a good idea but it was further explained that these beasts tend to live in the metal springs in the absence of any bedding. So trusting that the bugs had not migrated to the newly issued biscuits and, if they had they should be easy to ferret out anyway, it was off to do some cremating. I no longer remember whether it was paraffin or lighter fuel that was applied but whatever it was it did the trick.

Lye Mun barracks were handed over to the government in 1985 and eventually converted into the Lei Yue Mun Park and Holiday Village

[8] with facilities that include a riding school, tennis and basket ball courts and football pitches. The barrack rooms in which we were accommodated have been converted into living quarters for the holiday makers, now bed-bug free I would presume. Whenever I see such dramatic changes to a place that was the scene of so much fighting, bloodshed and bravery I do wonder if the present day occupants have any idea of what went on there not so very long ago. Believing that the Chinese have an inherent fear of ghosts I very much doubt if some of the older generation would be happy taking a holiday in such places.

In addition to now having decent living accommodation the move to Lye Mun was further welcomed by many as it was only a short walk down the hill to where one could take a tram ride into the centre of Victoria to avail themselves of all the usual facilities, including the various clubs catering for Britain's armed forces stationed there. Four such clubs were particularly popular, these being the Cheero (aka Cheerio) Club, the Catholic Club, as the name implies, run by the Catholic Church and serving the best steak egg and chips on the island. The China Fleet Club that was administered by the Royal Navy where many RN personnel were accommodated when their ships were in port. The Fleet Club itself had a large bar and a cinema and was open to all other members of the armed forces plus the crews of visiting United States Naval vessels. Just a short walk from the Fleet Club located on the main road there was the Sailors and Soldiers Club with a restaurant but under whose patronage I cannot at this stage remember. This latter club, known to all as the S and S, had a well deserved reputation for very fine sea-food meals and for serving some of the largest beef steaks to be had in the colony. There was also another club run by the YMCA but that was over in Kowloon on the mainland.

It is not possible for me to leave the mention of the Sailors and Soldiers club without referring to my very good friend John from my Boy Entrant days and with whom I was very lucky to be stationed with in Hong Kong. John, unlike myself, was very careful with money but I hasten to add was not stingy, far from it, in fact he was very generous.

He could, and probably still can, work wonders with a small amount of money. Early on at Lye Mun he suggested that we both retain one dollar (equivalent to one shilling and three pence in old money) of our fortnightly pay and blow it all the day before pay day.

As the tram terminus was just a short walk down the hill we could board a tram to take us into town for ten cents. Needing another ten cents for the return journey we were now left with the princely sum of eighty cents each. Now most people would probably quite rightly think that little could be obtained and enjoyed for such a small amount, not John. Alighting from the tram outside the Sailors and Soldiers club we would enter and enjoy a very nice salmon salad (the cheapest meal on the menu) which when paid for left us the few coins necessary for entry to the Fleet Club cinema and our return tram fare. A pleasant evening, a tram ride, a decent meal and a film for very little money and the next day was pay day anyway so we were never broke. I don't think anyone ever suggested that John should go into politics and go all out for the job of Chancellor of the Exchequer. I'm sure he could have made a better job of it than some we have had over the years; maybe it's not too late.

For most, myself included, providing we were not on watch on the evening of pay day usually meant a visit to the NAAFI to enjoy a few glasses of the famous San Miguel Pale Pilsner (pronounced Pilsen by the advertisers) with one's pals, generally from the same watch. More often than not such festivities took place seated outdoors, particularly on warm evenings of which there were many in Hong Kong. After a few pints of this thirst quenching beverage the singing would start, a variety of songs, mostly with a bawdy flavour. One feature of such musical renderings was that whatever the song was, it always seemed to end with a rousing chorus of something that went like;

Saaaaan Mig', Saaaaan Mig'

San Mig' is good enough for me.

Somehow I don't think the brewers were aware of how much their ale was appreciated and celebrated in song so often and so lustily by the loyal and often drunken sons of the British Empire. This brewery was the sponsor of music programmes listened to and enjoyed by the British Forces in that part of the world. The radio station broadcasting from Manila in the Philippines identified itself on the air as DZMB or being rather Americanised, Dee Zee Emm Bee Manila and liberally sprinkled its broadcasts with advertising slogans for the, already well familiar to us all, San Miguel Pale Pilsen.

Another lasting pleasant memory of our short stay at Lye Mun is of one of the lads I shared a billet or barrack room with. He was a tall Birmingham lad and I think a National Service airman. Every so often he would receive a large package from home and it was indeed large, about 35 x 20cm but not particularly deep. This lad, I'll call him Brummie which is probably what he was known as anyway, would eagerly open his parcel then wander around the room enquiring if anyone would like a piece of his mum's bread and butter pudding. He was so sincere and posing his question in a broad Birmingham accent (particularly the word pudding) one could hardly refuse. Having said that, very few people did refuse, I was always more than pleased to accept his kind offer and mum's bread and butter pudding was delicious even though it had taken weeks to arrive in Hong Kong from Birmingham by sea. Thank you Brummie, wherever you are.

Another occupant of that same barrack room was a tall Yorkshire lad, John Conboy who I believe was yet another National Service airman. John and I would often go on to the roof of the barrack block and spend time completing, or attempting to complete the cross-word puzzles in a weekly edition of a UK newspaper. Many years later watching the evening news bulletin on television when it was covering a murder enquiry in Leeds, the image of my former cross word puzzle companion appeared on the screen. I am always very pleased to see or hear of former colleagues that have done well after leaving the service and this one certainly had. I was especially pleased to see that the image I was then seeing of the senior police officer in charge of this case was no other than Detective Chief Superintendent John Conboy, previously known to me as Senior Aircraftman John Conboy, nice one John.

In early 1953, with the building work at Little Sai Wan completed, the temporary residents of Lye Mun were able to depart the bed bug infested blocks they had been 'enjoying' and sample the comfort of their new purpose built barrack blocks. No more bumpy rides to work in the back of a 3-ton truck or a march to work in the heat of the day as was sometimes the norm at Cape Collinson should such conveyance or driver not be available. This new accommodation was a vast improvement on that endured at Cape Collinson. Some of blocks themselves were of four-story construction with the accommodation on the top three floors similar to the three-story ones at Lye Mun but not in the old colonial style and therefore having a more modern look about them. The main difference for me however, was that the rooms on each floor were made to accommodate four airmen and therefore were not as 'airy' as the larger ones at Lye Mun accommodating at least eight or ten.

What did not improve however, was the food in the Airmen's Mess. The food at Cape Collinson had not been anything to write home about, except perhaps in a negative manner but on the new site it was at times just about inedible. Eventually, a few of the more daring, and possibly hungrier young lads, decided to mount a protest. This mutinous protest took the form of a parade around the site led by a well-built coloured lad from Glasgow chanting appropriate slogans relating to the food being served up in the airmen's mess. For most, if not all serving personnel at this time such behaviour, tantamount to mutiny, was unheard of. Only to be expected, the officers, no doubt tucking into their T-bone steaks and the like were astounded to say the least and the Station Commander was probably choking on his chips. With the arrival on the scene of the Flight Sergeant in charge of Discipline and Good Order, who also happened to be a Telegraphist, things quietened down and after the obvious questions as to what was going on and replies received, the Flight Sergeant, ordered them to disperse. Later in the day the station commander issued an order for all those involved in this 'near mutiny' to parade the following morning.

At the subsequent parade this station commander issued a severe bollocking to all present warning that any repetition would be treated most seriously and severe consequences would certainly follow. I would have thought that following what he had to say he could have issued an invitation to sit around the table and discuss the reasons for the protest in the first place and look for suggestions to avoid a recurrence. That, to my mind would have been the reasonable democratic thing to do. Unfortunately democracy, in those days was not on the agenda, in most disputes or disagreements that may have arisen. Should the discussion phase ever have been reached it would have been held in a 'them and us' atmosphere, we are in charge and when I shout jump you will shout, how high? On the way up. In the aftermath of this protest parade, who got the blame? The Senior NCOs of course, not the catering staff, those responsible for serving up the swill or whoever supplied poor quality raw ingredients for the cooks to perform miracles with. According to said Station Commander the Senior NCOs should have smartly exited their mess and nipped the protest in the bud. Other former members of the unit have memories of so-called 'Deaf' strikes but I personally had no experience of these. These strikes were also related to the poor quality of food in the mess. A number of operators would get together and simply refuse to hear what they were tasked to listen to during their watch. It was easy enough to do this simply by moving the tuning dial of their receiver slightly off the given frequency. Of course the supervisor could in turn monitor the frequency in use on his set and when a transmission was heard remonstrate with the operator that was supposed to be logging transmissions on that frequency. As far as I am aware no disciplinary action ever ensued. When word of the dissatisfaction regarding the catering and the consequent disruptive action appertaining to this eventually reached the ears of higher authority, which would have included GCHQ/DSD the quality of the food did improve, for a time at least. However, as I say, I never personally experienced this type of strike that, I believe, took place after I left Hong Kong in September 1953, there is no doubt however, that such token protests did take place.

Saying goodbye to Cape Collinson was not to be regretted apart from one facility there that was to be sadly missed by many. Just a 30 minute walk along the side of the surrounding hills one could arrive, albeit in a sweat, at Big Wave Bay that had a fine beach. This beach was used not only by the inhabitants of Cape Collinson but by many other Brits and their families on the Island so there was a sort-of back to normality feel about the place. I can't say that swimming at that location was always safe as there was at times a very strong undercurrent and I do remember on one occasion two of us having to help a colleague who got into difficulties. Apart from that many an impromptu game of cricket of sorts was to be enjoyed by some or one could simply do what one normally does on a beach, put the towel down and either sunbath or just relax.

There was another beach favoured by a few, just a short walk along the coast from Big Wave, known as Sheko. I no longer remember why some preferred Sheko to Big Wave although I did go there a few times. Perhaps the swimming was safer or there were more 'White Women' to be seen there, a rarity to young lads far from home. I would stress seen, but not touched. Most, but not the entire British civilian contingent in the Colony maintained a snobbish attitude towards what they regarded as common soldiers or servicemen. Not an attitude limited to Hong Kong however, it seems this was to be experienced in other parts of the world wherever British Servicemen were stationed and where there was also a British overseas civilian element. An attitude that was to change whenever there was a threatened or actual uprising of sorts and it fell to these servicemen to assist and provide the only means available to enable a rapid and safe evacuation of the Brits and their families be it by sea or by air.

I have often wondered just how many young lads took up the

habit of smoking at Cape Collinson as a result of the occasional free issue of cigarettes. Entering the airmen's mess for the evening meal one would sometimes find, at each place setting on the tables a sealed tubular tin of 50 cigarettes. The popular opinion was that these were formerly goods seized by HM Customs and instead of being destroyed they were issued to service personnel. How true this was I have no idea but it certainly seems plausible. In my memory the brand always seemed to be Senior Service but no doubt, if the Customs seizure theory is correct there were other brands on issue. I for one did indeed start to smoke cigarettes at this time but I am pleased to say that, apart from a couple of other short periods in my life, the habit was not continued.

The operational unit was staffed by RAF personnel, with a small contingent of RAAF (Royal Australian Air Force) personnel working eight-hour shifts. Their task was to monitor mainly Chinese Military, Chinese Naval Air Force and Chinese Air Force Morse code radio traffic. From a personal point of view the Military traffic was routine stuff and consisted of page upon page of Chinese short five figure groups, a simple task for any competent operator. The Chinese Air Force Morse traffic was somewhat more demanding and took the form of reports from ground radar stations. These stations would transmit a series of almost non-stop tracking reports at a rapid speed and also in the Chinese short form of figures. Such was the quantity and speed of this traffic that the operator having no time to insert carbons in his stack of message pads that were rapidly dwindling and needed replenishing, had to scream the word "pads". A supervisor or whoever nearby that may not have been very busy would oblige with a new supply of same.

In addition to a number of positions dedicated to the tasks described there were four or five positions in a separate room adjacent to the main operations or set room devoted to searching for new or previously unidentified transmissions. The name given to this operation was General Search (GS). Each operator would be given a frequency band to search. One operator would be tasked to search for example, 4 - 5 MHz and the next operator 5 - 6 MHz and so on so that the spectrum known to be most active in that part of the world during the day or night would be well covered. The operator was expected to find and log a transmission at least every fifteen minutes although not necessarily new or previously unidentified. More to see that he had not fallen asleep on the job I suppose. Operators so employed were the human equivalent of today's Automatic Radio Scanners that were yet to be invented. Positioned at a desk to the rear of these operators was a corporal supervisor with a comprehensive card-index system containing details, frequencies in use and call-signs used by all so far known active target stations. It would also contain details of transmissions from allied and friendly nations previously heard in order that should an operator intercept one of these it could be ignored as not required and he could quickly move on and continue to search his allotted band. It was the supervisor's job therefore to identify all the intercepts that the operator could not himself readily identify. From time to time a station that was already being monitored in the adjacent set room (operations room) would be logged. This usually happened when the transmission was intercepted whilst in the middle of a message in which case there would be no obvious indication as to its identity. Eventually it would of course be identified partially by the frequency and call-signs in use. In such cases the log would not be destroyed but would be used as a check and confirmation of what the other operator had logged. This would have been particularly useful during periods of poor reception when it would have been a case of believing that two heads are better than one. Not a lot of operators enjoyed the 'General Search' duty and preferred to monitor a particular station that they had become familiar with and knew what to expect. Personally, I enjoyed GS because there was variety and always the chance of finding something new or previously unidentified that did from time to time happen and had the lads working in TA (Traffic Analysis) running around in a state of some excitement.

The majority of radio receivers in use at that time were by no means modern. Many were receivers that had been in use during and since the end of WWII. In fairness however I must say that the main set in use, the National HRO was, in my opinion and indeed in the opinion of many others, the finest set of its time. Its only drawback was that in order to change to another frequency band one had first to remove the large coil pack from the front of the receiver, and exchange it with another from a box containing a number of such coil packs covering the HF (High Frequency) bands, that being 0 - 30 MHz. One could never be completely accurate as to exactly which frequency one was tuned to because there was no frequency read-out on the front of the receiver, just a large circular tuning dial and a number of other controls. On the front of the inserted coil there was a small graph indicating the frequencies covered by that particular pack, from that and by referring to the position of the marks on the tuning dial one could work out the approximate frequency to within a very few megacycles (these days always referred to as Megahertz) but it was rarely spot-on. A standard wave meter such as the BC221, used to measure the frequency could of course have been used and was so used on occasion but in those days such a bulky device was just not practical in a large operations room with so many sets. The only other set in use there at that time was the Marconi R1475, I believe designed for and used specifically by the military. One thing in its favour was its most accurate and easily read frequency display on its tuning dial.. Having this facility made it an ideal receiver for use in the General Search Role where the operator needed to report and log, as near as possible the exact frequency of his intercept. It was never my favourite though I have no idea why, I just never liked the feel of it, something only wireless operators will understand I suppose. The R1475 also had what was known as a 'Guard' channel where one could insert a crystal tuned to a particular frequency. This frequency would be one on which a required target was known to be only intermittently active so one was able to simultaneously use the set on other frequencies and be alerted when the frequency in the guard channel became active. A useful addition to have in certain circumstances but never, in my time, did I see it in use.

In the early 1950s an elderly Chinese cleaner, known to all as Pop, was employed to empty the waste bins and generally keep the set room tidy. This chap spoke no English but no doubt there were a number of printed words he was well familiar with such as Top Secret, Secret and Confidential, words he would quite possibly be on the look-out for among the waste. He could also be seen to actually lift an operators set of pads off the workspace in order to dust around them. Some time later during my service there this fellow was relegated to cleaning the small canteen when a more security conscious officer arrived on the scene and possibly threw a fit when he viewed the situation.

No. 367 Signals Unit had a small number of outstations, two in the New Territories, Tai Po Tsai and Ping Shan (the latter later renamed Kong Wei as there was an RAF Radar Station nearby with the name Ping Shan) and one up on Victoria Peak on the Island that went under the strange name of Batty's Belvedere. Some reports published on the internet show that it was RAF Chinese Linguists at Batty's but prior to the arrival of the first batch of Chinese linguists in Hong Kong there were a number of RAF Specialist (Morse) sigint operators working there and living in a block of apartments at North Point on the island.

Ping Shan, in the New Territories, within sight of Communist China was a small HFDF (High Frequency Direction Finding) unit in support of the main unit at Little Sai Wan. The DF hut itself was sited in the middle of a Padi [9] (rice) field and was surrounded by a wooden fence. Transport would drop the ongoing shift off and collect the off-going watch on the main road a couple of hundred metres from the hut. After being dropped off one would then make ones way to the hut along a narrow path of which there were many. Unfortunately such paths were not entirely solid as small culverts were dug beneath them in places to facilitate channelling of the water, in which the rice was planted so one had to be extra careful if one wanted to avoid a soaking.

In order to sustain ourselves when on duty in this remote outpost we would bring our daily or nightly rations with us, usually sandwiches and some fruit. This fare was conveniently carried in a small hand-carried wicker hamper of the type so popular in the Far East. On one particular evening our Australian member of the team, 'Donkey' (we never did learn his given name) Burrows wasn't careful enough and took a dive into the Padi taking with him the night's rations. I was one of the off-going watch on this occasion and as Donkey approached the hut he was laughing his head off, as we met him at the door, he, still laughing but very wet blurted out, "I dropped the fackin' tacker". Not the slightest bit bothered that he would have to sit the watch out starkers until his uniform dried out, he was more concerned about the 'Tucker'. A typical easy-going Aussie and a very popular likeable colleague. Going off watch and our transport waiting on the road, we didn't wait to find out just how much 'tucker' was salvageable but some of it must have been as both 'Donkey' and his companion on the night watch were none the worse the next morning, except perhaps a little hungrier than usual.

Power to operate the Marconi Adcock DF system was drawn from 12-volt truck batteries two of which were continually on charge using small JAP[10] engines. This charging facility was located to the rear of the hut, perilously close to the Jerry cans holding the petrol supply for the tiny engines. In inclement weather, an engine and one of the batteries were removed to the small 'Privy' or 'Thunderbox' in the corner of the compound. Problems only arose with these arrangements when anyone needed to use the facilities. At such times this person sat on the throne with feet up on the little engine, his whole body vibrating madly to the rhythm of the engine. An added hazard of course were the fumes, mainly, but not entirely, from the engine thereby forcing the occupant to leave the 'Privy' door open whilst communing with Mother Nature. Fortunately the operators did not have the unpleasant task of disposing of the contents of the bucket; this was done by a Night Soil Coolie who lived in a nearby village. This fellow had a vegetable patch in the padi field a short distance to the rear of the DF hut where he cultivated some fine tomatoes. And particularly fine they were considering what he used as a fertilizer. He would frequently offer us some of his tomatoes but, having been continually advised via SROs [11] (Station Routine Orders) not to eat such local fare, we had to politely refuse. We would often pass the time of the day with this gentleman who, surprisingly enough was not Chinese but was an Australian Aborigine. In his younger days he had spent some time as a merchant seaman and having met a Chinese girl when in port in Hong Kong he decided to stay. This was one Aborigine that really went 'Walk About'. He had settled down well and we assumed that his wife was the same young lady he had first met. His English was comical, typical of what we thought was the norm for an Aborigine, never having previously met one but had seen and heard such fellows only in films. During conversation many of the words he used would end in 'um', eat-um, like-um, bring-um and a sprinkling of Anglo Saxon swear words similarly suffixed.

Sometimes, in the late afternoon prior to the watch changeover with the other operator on the set I would take a short walk across the padi. About 200 metres from the hut there was a small fast running stream, something like what we would call a brook or a beck in England. I would sit on a rock alongside this stream and watch with fascination the behaviour of a small very slim snake. At this point the stream would flow over some small rocks and have the appearance of a mini waterfall. Small fish would try, and sometime succeed in leaping over this waterfall and then continue up-stream. A number of these tiny fish would however, fail to complete the leap. The snake would position itself motionless, partially in the stream with its head raised and at the right moment catch a fish neatly mid leap. I would leave this spot happy in the knowledge that I had been privileged to witness an interesting event in the natural world.

Well into the watch one night, approximately fifteen minutes after one of the JAP engines had been refuelled the occupants had to hastily exit the hut as it burst into flames. Fire was not the only hazard however, the .303 rifle ammunition started to explode and as debris was flying everywhere the two unfortunates on watch had to lie down in the Padi field out of harms way. Presumably the flames were visible from the nearby village and eventually help arrived as the fire burnt itself out.

The cause of the fire was deemed to have been caused by a fault that had developed in one of the JAP engines resulting in the ignition of its petrol supply and eventually the fuel in the adjacent Jerry Cans as they exploded in the heat. The Hut and all the equipment in it, including the rifles, the watch keeper's only defence against Chairman Mao's millions across the way, was destroyed. Luckily, the two occupants of the hut that night survived unscathed if somewhat damp following their prone visit to the Padi.

A new DF site was later built some short distance away alongside the road. This was an all 'Singing and Dancing' job with a beautifully made copper earth mat and two large diesel powered generators housed in a purpose built shed. Everything nice and modern, indeed almost posh enough for a civilian Radio Operator although I doubt if that ever happened in its early days. It certainly would not have taken place in the old hut in the middle of the padi field without a massive 'hardship' allowance being sanctioned. The six airmen (five RAF and one RAAF) plus a Corporal employed at Ping Shan were accommodated at RAF Sek Kong some five miles (8Kms) or so further north. For these souls it was back to Nissan huts once more. Strangely enough, such billets as they were felt somewhat more comfortable than those previously experienced at Cape Collinson. The particular hut occupied by the 367 Signals Unit detachment was shared with a small number of other airmen, one at least working at the aforementioned Radar Station and others at an R/T DF (Radio Telephony Direction Finding) hut perched atop a hill about four kilometres to the west of Ping Shan and close to the coast. The purpose of this outpost being to provide information in the form of directional guidance (bearings) to the de Havilland Vampire fighter aircraft of No.28 Squadron based at Sek Kong. Other occupants of the Nissan hut at Sek Kong were two or three Royal Artillery soldiers who operated an Army PPI (Plan Position Indicator) Radar that served as a GCA (Ground Control Approach) unit on the airfield. The same Aborigine chap was also employed here to 'service' the thunder box toilet facilities of which there were many, presumably this is where he had learnt his English swear words.

The catering arrangements at Sek Kong were well short of being Cordon Bleu. The cook in the airmen's' mess, which was really just another, but somewhat larger, Nissan hut, was a large rough and ready fellow whose hygiene may have been somewhat lacking but I don't think anyone's well-being ever seriously suffered from digesting his offerings. As far as I can remember, the meals turned out in his kitchen could never be called exotic but were always wholesome and satisfying, certainly I never heard anyone complain of being hungry.

On a table, outside the dining hall, yes another large Nissan hut, were three identical stainless steel buckets. One contained hot water for washing ones 'irons' (knife fork and spoon), and one for rinsing those implements. The third one contained a scalding hot brew of tea in to which one dipped one's, usually enamel, mug to take said brew back to the billet to enjoy. No choice of with or without sugar or milk of course. One evening my pal there almost caused a riot when chatting away to me and not looking what he was doing rinsed his washed but not yet rinsed irons in the tea bucket, the meal had been one of fish that evening which could have made matters worse. The lads in the queue behind him were not well pleased but in the end, not detecting any fish debris in the tea, saw the funny side of it.

Attending to our needs in the way of laundering, ironing our clothes and keeping the hut swept and tidy was our Amah, Ping. An ever smiling and cheerful Chinese lady who sometimes brought her little girl Sue to work with her. One day Ping asked if she could have the next day off, when asked the reason for the request she said simply, "to have a baby". That was all she wanted, one day, no maternity leave and pampering for Ping. Of course the services of our Amah were not free nor were they paid for by the RAF. I can't be absolutely sure now but I think the amount each occupant of the hut was required to pay her was HK$2, two shillings and sixpence per fortnight in old money, not a fortune but to dear Ping it must have represented a fair wage.

The gallant leader of this merry band, the corporal, for much of my time there was one Michael (Mick) Brophy a jovial Irishman and quite a character. The Royal Air Force in my time seemed to have many characters among its ranks, the sort of person that one never forgets and who always seems to get a mention when old comrades are gathered together. Mick Brophy was one such a person. Single, and when off duty hell bent on enjoying himself and making sure those around him did the same. At work, he was always conscientious and dedicated to the job in hand but outside the working environment a different person. He knew all the best bars and other watering holes in the colony and was always happy to introduce any newcomer to them.

The Corporals' Club at Sek Kong was located in another Nissan hut close to our billets. It was in here that Mick and his fellow corporals would make merry during some of their free time but Mick always seemed to be the star of the show. On one occasion with a party underway, he walked in to the club leading a mule. There was an army unit on Sek Kong that took care of a number of mules used to transport ammunition to an artillery unit up in the hills. Mick simply borrowed one and took it for a walk taking it into the Corporals' Club as though it was a normal everyday thing to do. The mule was made a fuss of by the gathering and then returned unharmed, if maybe somewhat puzzled, to the safety of its quarters. I have, in recent years, spoken to friends who have had access and invites to social events at present day RAF stations and they all say that the service is just not the same and no longer seems to have any real 'characters', more's the pity. Mick and I were to meet up again some years later in the UK and were by then, both members of the Sergeants' Mess at RAF Wythall and later, RAF Digby, he hadn't changed. He never did drive but when at Digby, as I had a car he would sometimes persuade me and a few others to go off and visit some of the pubs in the Lincolnshire countryside. My memory tells me that most of these pubs had pretty smiling barmaids. Mick would always be the first to front up to the bar and introduce himself and his companions, I was always introduced as the Racing Correspondent of the Catholic Herald, such was his humour. Sadly, Mick was to die in a road traffic accident in the UK in 1964 and is buried in a tiny cemetery in the village of Scopwick close to RAF Digby.

By the very nature of things, personnel reaching their 'Tour Expired' date or being returned to Little Sai Wan for one reason or another meant that I had from time-to-time new faces to share the duties with. One fellow in particular didn't stay long; he had fallen madly in love with a Chinese lady and applied to his Commanding Officer for permission to marry. Such permission was not given lightly and the intended spouse in this case was 'investigated' with the result that permission was refused. It transpired that allegedly, the said lady was considered extremely undesirable. However, this particular colleague who, incidentally was very diligently teaching himself Chinese, was not content to leave it at that and protested loudly still stating his intention to marry the light of his life. It seems that the authorities were having none of this and quickly removed him from sigint duties by posting him to Singapore. That was not however, the last we were to hear of the matter as still protesting he wrote to one of the UK Sunday Newspapers, one no longer in print, the *People* I think it was. The story actually made a splash with large headlines. Good copy for the newspaper, a sob story of the type, 'The RAF refuses to let me marry' etc but it did the chap no good except perhaps he received a small monetary reward from the newspaper for his efforts. One other operator that happened upon us and I remember little about him except that he was from Manchester and possibly a National Service Airman. Why I mention him though is that he was often heard to make the statement; "If there is another war I shall head for the Yorkshire Moors and hide out there". A fine sentiment but not very patriotic. If everyone had that idea maybe there would be no more wars because there would be no one around to fight but the Yorkshire Moors would become rather overcrowded.

Our system of telecommunication with the parent unit at Little Sai Wan was rather primitive. We obviously required some form of contact as Sai Wan needed to let us know with some degree of urgency when they wanted a bearing taken on a particular transmission that they were hearing. This requirement was passed to us by what was little more than a Field Telephone where one wound the handle and hoped for a reply. Such instruments are not intended for anything but short distances but it seems that they did a sterling job in the trenches in WWI. This one was routed all the way to Little Sai Wan using some form of amplifiers and maintained by a British Army Unit on the island. It was often very hit and miss and not infrequently out of service. One particular night when on watch and I had for some time been trying to contact Sai Wan and was hearing only what I presumed to be the army engineers working on the line I finally made contact. On being asked what the delay was I said something like, "been trying to get through for ages but there was some Pongo[12] on the line". Immediately a cultured Hooray Henry sounding voice I had previously been hearing came on the line, "It was not a Pongo, this is Lieutenant ....of the Royal Corps of Signals". Oops! I heard no more about this; maybe the Lieutenant should not have been listening in to my conversation with Sai Wan.

I would like to think that we were a happy bunch at Sek Kong Certainly we were never bothered by the authorities there. We were simply treated as what we were, lodgers, and allowed to get on with the job. During my time at Sek Kong we always enjoyed each other's company both on and off duty. We would often go off walking in the surrounding hills or enjoy a spot of fishing in the nearby river with the other RAF and Army occupants of the billet. Sadly however, as is often the case someone will spoil the party. This fellow was a West Indian. PC forbids me to refer to him with the no longer heard or used phrase that comes to mind but he really did turn out to be the 'the person in the supply of wood'. He simply did not fit in, when on night watch it was usual for one of the two on duty, now in the new site with diesel generators, to attend to the refuelling of such. The generator would be shut down whilst it was refuelled then had to be re-started. Whenever it was this fellow's turn to carry out this procedure he would often return to the hut complaining that the generator would not re-start and when attempting to do so it would start to surge. That meant quite simply, no power so no work and one could get ones head down for the night. The ploy never worked because the other watch keeper would manage to re-start the generator. Two words sum this fellow up, Idle Sod.

Waking one morning one of my colleagues discovered that his wallet, which in common with the rest of us he normally left on his bedside locker, was missing and this the day following pay day. It was certainly not likely that we would have had an intruder, that just did not happen and anyone intent on entering the billet and robbing would have helped himself to more than one person's belongings. No accusations were made; being of a comradely nature we all trusted each other. Only one person was absent when this discovery was made and he had left to go on watch alone [13] early that morning and would not return until relieved the same evening.

Shortly after going on watch that evening the two lads were alerted by someone shouting to them from the nearby road. This turned out to be a Chinese fellow who kept his small flock of tiny ducks in the waters of the padi field surrounding the hut. In order to keep his ducks together and to recover any that may be tempted to stray he was armed with a long bamboo pole that had a wire loop on one end. When one of the lads on watch went to see what the fuss was about he was greeted with the sight of this gent holding one very wet wallet containing only the form F1250 (Service Identity Card) of our colleague who was missing his. There are no prizes for guessing how that wallet came to be in the padi field when only one of our colleagues had been on watch that day. Friendly honest Chinese duck-keeper had fished said wallet out of the water with his bamboo pole.

The matter was reported to the officer in nominal charge of us back at Little Sai Wan who for reasons best known to himself did not take the action one would expect. This would have been to directly charge the culprit with the offence of stealing from his comrades. Instead this undesirable was, without further delay posted to the station signals centre at RAF Kai Tak, the RAF and Civil airport in Hong Kong. Some months later I was to meet the Corporal in charge of the small signals centre there, a fellow ex-boy. He informed me that our former thieving colleague had got himself into further trouble of a similar nature at Kai Tak and had been severely and justly dealt with.

Some of my off-duty time in the colony when based on the island was spent playing rugby, a game I had been introduced to during my boy's service and which I was to enjoy playing (not particularly well) for a good number of years. My first game, shortly after arriving in Hong Kong was to result in my one and only spell of jankers whilst there. As is often the case following a game, most of the team, particularly the unmarried members, would take themselves off and enjoy a few drinks in one or more of the many bars. In Hong Kong, where there were bars there were bar girls. After a few pints of the amber liquid all these 'bar girls' looked like every man's dream of an oriental beauty and became most desirable and obtainable, at a price.

For the first six months or so of ones tour there was a restriction with regard to when one had to be back in camp each evening, in my case the deadline was midnight. I'm afraid that on my first venture into the fleshpots of Hong Kong all thought of being back in camp by midnight went out of the window. On my, late the next morning, return to camp I was duly charged, and subsequently appeared before the unit commander where I was 'awarded' five days confined to camp (Jankers). I never did seem to get into any bother after this though as within about one year I was promoted to Corporal, became much wiser, and could stay out all night anyway. I just love that term 'awarded'. In the armed forces one was always 'awarded' punishment, as though one was being awarded or decorated with a medal. Using such terminology however, didn't make one feel any better about the situation. I still remember the name of the Corporal on duty in the Guard Room when I returned to camp and whose duty it was to place me on a charge, Corporal Chapel, somewhat older than most corporal policemen I knew or had known, an ex-Palestine Policeman and a nice chap. He was just doing what he was being paid to do and didn't seem to enjoy such minor routine work. I held no grudge.

One young colleague suffered an unfortunate turn of fate having succumbed to the charms of a particularly attractive Suzy Wong one night. First however, we must hark back to our days when training to be

45

Telegraphists. Not everyone found it easy to learn the Morse code or some of the other skills necessary to qualify in the trade. In a number of such cases the young trainee would apply to re-muster or transfer to another trade in which he thought he could do better and still remain in the RAF. Some did indeed do well having found their niche in life. A few come to mind, one lad who seemed to spend more time in the Station Sick Quarters (medical centre/hospital) than in the classroom re-mustered to the trade of Nursing Attendant and did well. Another became an Armourer, I don't know how well he did but from what I remember about him he would never have made out as a Telegraphist. Yet another, a very bright lad re-mustered to Aircrew as a pilot and also did very well. However, the one we are concerned about here became an SP, a Service Policeman, these days more often referred to as RAF Police or more informally as Snowdrops because of the white cover they wore on their peaked caps, in contrast to the red cap covers worn by the Army or Military Police. Most Service Policemen in my day were appointed to the rank of Acting Corporal (unpaid) together with the two stripes of the rank, known jocularly as 'Protection' Stripes, simply to give them the authority needed to carry out their duties. This particular Boy Entrant must have been an exception and quite a bright lad as once in the Police trade he very soon achieved the rank of Sergeant. So, to the tale of my colleague and his oriental maiden of the night. No doubt enjoying himself when the flimsy door of the 'Shack' burst open and in strode a Corporal SP. What the lad was up to was in no way an offence, the offence related to where he was, which was in one of the many 'Out of Bounds' areas on the island. These areas or districts were frequently patrolled by the police services of all the three British armed forces stationed in the colony. My quick thinking colleague immediately assumed an indignant posture and challenged the Corporal with "what the hell do you think you are doing?". The Corporal, not now sure of his ground asked the lad for his ID, "Bugger off" came the reply "I'm a Merchant Seaman, nothing to do with you lot". Corporal, now less sure of his ground, thought he would trip the lad up and asked, "Oh yes, and what ship are you on?" Quick as a flash the lad replied, "I am a baker on the Empire Pride". This vessel was a troopship currently berthed in the harbour. We were always aware of the arrival of troopships in port, mainly due to them bringing new arrivals to swell our numbers. The Corporal was about to turn on his heel and leave the room when in walked his Sergeant who, espying my colleague said, in a loud surprised voice, "Hello Carruthers", (not his real name). By an unfortunate turn of fate the Sergeant was the very one who myself and the other ex-boys stationed in Hong Kong knew very well, as he likewise knew us from those days some three years previous when we had all been trainees together. The lad was duly charged with being in an out of bounds area contrary to SROs and was, yes, 'awarded' a period of Jankers. The phrase 'How unlucky can you get' comes to mind here.

It is very easy to stand in judgement and criticise these young women, or more often just girls, and their young, far from home for the first time in their life, servicemen 'clients' but the situation those females found themselves in during the early fifties was an extremely desperate one. Between 1949 and 1951 the population of Hong Kong had dramatically increased with the flood of refugees from Communist China. More than half of the colony's, by then, more than two million souls, were squeezed on to the Island alone in an area of a little more than 31 square miles. So-called Slum Dwellings, known to us as Shacks were springing up all over the place. These shacks in many cases were built or more correctly knocked together from whatever the unfortunate refugees could find, a collection of large square biscuit tins opened up and flattened out to make the outside walls were very much in evidence. It was in this atmosphere that so many young women were desperate just to stay alive. A number of them had at least one young child that had to be cared for .Employment for the poorly or completely uneducated among them was impossible to find so they took the only road they could. Many of them would ply their trade as bar girls taking their clients to a small hotel. Some, particularly the most attractive ones would become 'employees' in a brothel of sorts, usually just an extension or upper floor of a bar. Others, mainly the younger ones would patrol or hang around close to where they knew members of the British Armed Forces would frequent and hope to 'pick up' a client. The young ladies in this latter category would not dress or have the appearance of the prostitutes we are now used to seeing in films or on our TV screens, heavily made up, wearing short skirts, very high-heeled shoes or leather boots etc. They would most likely be dressed Western style in a simple cotton frock and have the appearance of the girl next door. Most of these girls had never even been in a bar let alone worked in one and these were the unfortunates that lived in shacks. Like many things in life, circumstances dictate the way we live so we must not, in my opinion, for what it's worth, be too harsh or quick to criticise others less fortunate than ourselves.

Another form of popular pleasurable entertainment were the Taxi Dances, less risqué and less risky, in fact no risk that I was aware of was involved. On entering the dance hall one could almost imagine being in a dance hall in the UK, or at least in England, in the 1950s. This of course except for the fact that here all the young ladies seated like wallflowers around the periphery were Chinese and, in the main very attractive. Another big difference being that before the budding Fred Astaire could choose a partner and demonstrate his prowess, or lack of it, on the dance floor he had to purchase a number of tickets. One ticket, one dance was the rule and the young lady would cash her tickets in at the end of the night. At least this way, providing one purchased enough tickets one could play the field and dance with every girl in the hall for little more than a few Hong Kong dollars. Dancing was all that was allowed, these girls were not prostitutes although it was said that some could be bought for the night by paying the dance hall owner a fixed sum of money. I was never to put this to the test so am unable to substantiate this claim. I knew of one lad, a few years older than most of us, that had a long-term girl friend who he had met at a taxi dance hall. I presume he paid the owner for one night's company of the young lady then they came to some mutual arrangement. I know for sure that they did stay faithful to each other for his entire time in the colony and during this time she did not return to the dance hall.

In the 1950s a prerequisite for promotion to Corporal was the successful completion of a GDT (Ground Defence Training) course. The Far Eastern venue for this course that I was to attend was Diatalawa in northern Ceylon (Sri Lanka). Being selected to attend this course in 1952 I was pleased, for two reasons. One, unlike some of my comrades I never passed up the chance to 'play soldiers' and I knew that much of this was involved in the GDT course. Two, I would get to see yet another part of the world where I had previously only visited the country's capital, Colombo, when en-route to the Far East on the good ship Lancashire.

The course consisted of all the activities and the practising of skills that one would expect. Small arms firing, stripping and cleaning of same which at that time were the .303 calibre Le Enfield Rifle, the Bren Light-Machine Gun, the 9mm Sten Sub-Machine Gun and the Hand Grenade or Mill's Grenade Type 36 Mk I to give it its full title. Also included in the course curriculum was the requirement to stand up in front of other members of the course in a classroom and give a talk on a subject of ones own choosing.

The subject I chose to speak on was fishing. Not what is to me though, the boring practice of sitting on a canal bank all day, relaxing though it may be, nor the skilful art of fly fishing. My talk was on a number of illegal ways to catch a trout. Skills I had learned as a young boy from my neighbour and very good friend in North Wales. This neighbour at that time was an Air Gunner in the RAF and had gone through the war as a Tail Gunner on Lancaster Bombers. He was also an accomplished poacher, skills he had learned from his father and was happy to pass on to me. The methods I described, in addition to taking the trout from beneath a rock or large stone by hand were as follows. Taking the trout that was lying between the roots of a tree at the edge of the riverbank by the use of a fork stolen from Mum's cutlery drawer. First flatten the fork with a hammer, sharpen the prongs with a file and cut a small notch or barb in each prong then fasten the completed implement to a short piece of stick with strong twine. Insert this four-pronged spear very gently into the water above the head of the fish then quickly plunge it down. If all had been properly assembled then you would be enjoying a nice trout for your next meal. One other method was to take a rabbit snare that normally has eight wound strands of fine copper wire. Unwind it and separate the strands, take one single strand about 4 or 5 feet in length from which to fashion a small noose at one end. Attach this to a long stick this time so that it has the appearance of a normal rod and line used for fishing. To use this one has to find a bridge or similar structure over a trout stream where trout (and sometimes Grayling) may be seen. Then all one has to do is gently immerse the noose upstream of the target and allow it to flow over head of the fish, just behind the gills whereupon you give it a sharp tug and again you have your dinner. I think I got thus far in my talk when the instructor said, "OK that's enough". Without thinking, as I was in full flow by this time I said, "But I haven't finished", "no, but I have" was the sharp reply. I guess he must have been a conventional Fly Fisherman and wanted to hear no more of my naughty stories even though my comrades on the course seemed to be hanging on my every word.

The 'playing soldiers' part of the course was fine until it came to the session where we were told to pair off, get camouflaged and disappear into the jungle. Fine if one chose the right spot which my partner, a small wiry lad from Paisley, and I on this occasion failed to do. The outcome was initially to feel very itchy, first of all around the ankles then in other delicate parts of the body. Not wanting to move and give our position away we stuck it out for a while but eventually had to investigate and discovered a number of leeches, by this time bloated from feeding on our lifeblood. These blighters before feeding can be thinner than a matchstick and as some readers will know can find their way to warm flesh even through the lace holes in ones boots. As neither of us, at this time, were cigarette smokers we could not perform the usual practice of burning these pests off with the lighted tip of a cigarette. We simply had to do what everyone is told not to do, resort to pulling them off. We had not yet learned of the trick of carrying a phial of iodine in one's ammunition pouches, allegedly a spot of such medication will quickly make the leech let go.

Part way through the course word was received that an aircraft had gone down in the jungle a good half day's journey away. So, under the guidance of two instructors the entire course piled into a 3-Ton truck and headed off to where this alleged incident had taken place. Arriving in the region in the late afternoon and making enquiries with the locals we were soon to realise that none of them seemed to know anything at all about a crashed aircraft. The questioning of these locals continued for a while once we ascertained that we were in the right place but the result remained the same. One lad, tongue well in cheek wanted to ask the question in halting English, 'did you see large silver bird fall from sky' but he was dissuaded by one of the more sensible members of the course. Nevertheless it may well have given us all a laugh as by this time it looked very much like we had been on a false errand and were becoming quite fed up. To make matters worse our leaders decided that we must stay the night in this area. Permission was obtained to sleep in a large building used as a store for huge slabs of latex or rubber. The smell from this was enough alone to interfere with ones slumbers but the place was infested with mosquitoes, there must have been squadrons of them. I know I got no sleep whatsoever and neither, I believe, did many others. So it was a weary and somewhat unkempt mob that boarded the truck early next morning to return to Diatalawa and enjoy a hearty breakfast meal. I have often wondered since if the tale of the downed aircraft was not a ruse by some of the locals in that area to have a party of British servicemen go to their area and part with a few rupees. Not that there was much in evidence worth spending money on except a sort of soft drinks stall which did in fact do a roaring trade.

Yet another enjoyable part of this course was the Escape and Evasion exercise. We were all taken by a 3-ton truck, and dropped, in pairs at various points some miles from the camp. The instructions were to make ones way back to camp. In essence we were to play at POWs (Prisoners of War) having escaped from captivity and making our way home. We were informed that enemy guards, in the form of the school's instructional staff, would be out there to (they hoped) intercept and capture us somewhere between where we were dropped off and our destination.. Should we be captured then we had failed in this particular exercise. We were dropped off early in the morning and given until midnight that day to complete the task, one way or another.

My partner for this exercise was an Irish lad but I don't at this stage remember much else about him. We found ourselves on some high ground above a tea plantation where a number of ladies and young girls in brightly coloured saris and such like were picking tea. Below this plantation we could see a railway line that immediately gave us an idea of how to get back to camp the easy way without being caught, take the train of course. We had not been allowed to carry money on this exercise so the case of buying tickets was out of the question and there was no station in sight anyway. As the line was, at this point, on an uphill gradient and on a slight bend it seemed a likely place to enable us to grab hold and hang on. As luck would have it we did not have to wait long before we heard the approach of the steam driven conveyance that would help us fool our instructors, get back to camp early and put our feet up for the remainder of the day. There we were, poised like a couple of coiled springs waiting to pounce when the train reached us. It did and we didn't, pounce that is. Our idea that said locomotive would only be chugging along at this point was misconceived, it wasn't exactly out to break any speed records but was fast enough to tear our arms out of their sockets if we had tried to grab on to any of it's protrusions. Mad idea abandoned we tramped along the line for maybe a couple of miles and spotted a road that had possibilities. So idea number two was born, hitch a lift. The first vehicle that happened along was a large truck, not unlike the 3-ton Bedford that we had been dropped off from that very morning except that this one was not quite as pristine as our Air Force issue transport and somewhat slightly dilapidated. Not to be put off however, each with one arm in the air thumbs in evidence and with a hopeful look on our faces, when to our surprise the truck came to a halt. A question was put to the driver as to his destination. I no longer remember where he was heading but the name of the place sounded familiar and he said he would be pleased to give us a lift. So, around to the rear of the vehicle to find it already full of native labourers, all chatting and grinning as they helped us on board. We were dropped off just a short distance from the camp and were happy to walk the rest of the way. We were unsure as to what awaited us on our arrival but were pleasantly surprised to find that it was only necessary to 'log in' by signing a book and the locally enlisted policeman entered the time against our signatures. There was no sign of the 'enemy' who at this early stage had probably not even set out to intercept the escapees.

We all assembled the following morning to hear the results of the exercise. Names and times of return to base were read out. My partner and I were the first home but instead of being congratulated we were accused of cheating. The winning pair were a couple who did it the hard way and even claimed to have enjoyed it, arriving back shortly before midnight exhausted. I can't see how we cheated, surely escaped POWs are supposed to use their initiative to achieve their aim, be it by fair means or foul. That is exactly what we did but it seems that we were supposed to sweat it out. We came in for a good deal of abuse from the other course members but most of it good-natured. Some of them even said that they wished they had done the same, they had not enjoyed slogging on for miles in the tropical heat and humidity.

We were, as is normal practice in the East, afforded the services of a native bearer, a servant who kept our billet tidy, made the beds and gave the place a daily sweep. One morning he didn't show up but it was not long before the reason for his absence became obvious when a number of the lads discovered to their horror that they were missing their wallets containing what few rupees they had. The local police were called in as a matter of course but it seemed that the villain was not to be found, he had simply disappeared from his village and apparently no one had any idea where he had gone. No more was heard of the matter and it was put down to experience. Most members of the course were, like myself, stationed at other locations throughout the Far East where they had female Amahs to attend to their domestic chores. Never in my time, in Hong Kong or Singapore did I come across any thieving by these employees and they were always trusted by the billet's occupants, even to the degree that some would leave their wallets either on top of their bedside lockers or inside the locker that more often than not was left unlocked. Obviously such trust could not be displayed in Ceylon.

I have never had any great interest in the game of cricket and certainly had never seriously played it until attending this course in Sri Lanka, if one can call a three-minute innings playing that is. One other member of the course, I think the same lad that was with me on the escape and evasion exercise decided, or perhaps someone had decided for us that we needed a haircut and as there was a local barber employed on the camp we proceeded to pay him a visit. Sitting on our chairs awaiting our turn when in walked an RAF PTI (Physical Training Instructor). Addressing the assembled barber's shop clients he shouted, (members of that calling cannot talk, they always shout) "Anyone play Cricket"?. A deathly silence ensued so this fellow turned to my companion and I saying, "OK, you two will do, let's have you outside". So, being good obedient airmen we followed him outside, we didn't have a lot of choice really as even though he was a mere corporal he outranked us. Outside there was a game of cricket in progress, it was explained to us that this was a match between RAF Diatalawa and an XI of the Royal Ceylon Air Force (RCyAF, founded in 1951). All the players in sight were resplendent in their lovely white cricket togs whereas we were in the dress of the day for the course, denims, or as our American counterparts would call them, fatigues. Within a few short minutes the PTI told us that the RAF team were a couple of players short so we would have to make up the numbers, with that I found myself strapped into a pair of large white pads, having a bat thrust into my hand and being told, "your on, get out there." So out to the wicket I strode trying to look as though I knew what I was doing. Taking a stance at the crease and looking nervously at the fellow who was about to hurl a very hard solid object in my direction and thinking, now he does look as though he knows what he's doing.. Hurl the object he did, I don't think I saw it but certainly felt it when it hit me fair and square on the left shoulder. A couple of players ran toward me, including the one who had hurled the offending missile, saying "are you all right". Of course I was all right; I was still vertical so the game continued. The next ball, which I also don't remember seeing, splattered my wicket. Oh joy! I was out and allowed to make my way back to the barber's shop with a bruise that I did not have when I set out that day to have a haircut. No doubt somewhere in the history of RAF Diatalawa my name is inscribed in the records of the cricket team there as being 'out for duck' in a game against the Royal Ceylon Air Force, fame indeed. I don't remember now how the other lad faired apart from not being hit by the first ball aimed at him, or more likely aimed at his wicket, and staying at the crease somewhat longer than I.

The journey to and from Ceylon was made aboard a Vickers Valetta, the RAF's replacement for the ubiquitous Dakota or Douglas DC3. As this aircraft required one or more refuelling stops for the Hong Kong - Ceylon journey it gave me the opportunity to see, albeit briefly, a couple of other places I had hitherto never visited, one with an exotic sounding name, Car Nicobar, the northernmost island of the Nicobar group in the Indian Ocean. Prior to 2004 few people had heard of Car Nicobar but on 26 December that year it was all but wiped out when a tsunami struck, resulting in the loss of many lives, mainly Indian Air Force personnel and their families. When I was privileged to visit this tiny Island in 1952 it was an RAF Staging Post. I duly disembarked along with all the other passengers and the refuelling of the aircraft got underway. We were shepherded to a small hut expecting to be offered a cold drink to slake our thirst but oh no, this was not to be, we were given a difficult to hold paper cup of scalding hot tea for which we even had to sign!

One other refuelling stop, one that included an overnight stay and in complete contrast to Car Nicobar was Clark Field, a huge USAF base on the Philippine Island of Luzon. Dinning in a large mess hall we were to experience a number of dishes never before seen and certainly never served up in RAF dining halls in those days. Taking our well-laden plates through the serving area the chef behind the counter, who was able to see by our uniforms that we were Brits in transit, asked if we would like a pot of tea, adding that he had been given the recipe by an Englishman some time ago! This certainly brought a smile to our faces, never having heard of a recipe for Britain's favourite brew. None of us fancied a drink of tea at that time so we thanked him but politely declined his offer. Now if it had been scalding hot tea in a paper cup we might have, err, no I don't think so. We were not into drinking wine in those days, I don't think any of us had ever had the opportunity, it was not available anyway so I think we settled for a glass of iced water. Why does everyone think that because we are British we love a drink of tea? I hate the stuff. I didn't always of course; I used to enjoy a cuppa but just went off it overnight.

During the early fifties the RAF trade structure underwent a change. Now instead of being a Telegraphist, the trade I had trained for, I became a Telegraphist II (A) in the trade scale of 'Skilled'. The (A) indicating that I was also a qualified intercept operator. Should I wish to become an 'Advanced' tradesman (more pay) then I would have to undergo another course of training at No.3 Radio School, Compton Bassett in Wiltshire where I had undergone and completed my initial training. I didn't have a lot of choice in the matter. Three months prior to the completion of my tour of duty in Hong Kong I was told to pack and sent on my merry way to the UK to attend the six months course that, when completed, would make me a Telegraphist I (A).

I remember very little about the return journey to the UK. It was certainly by an RAF aircraft, a Handley Page Hastings. Most personnel were, at this time still being returned to the UK by sea but as the few of us on this trip were returning not tour-expired but to attend a course of instruction we had the relative luxury of a shorter passage by air.

This being prior to the jet-age of travel our trusty piston-engined Hastings required a number refuelling stops en-route. It's almost certain that we re-fuelled at Changi, Singapore but I have no recollection of this. Only three other stops now come to mind, the first one, Karachi in Pakistan, unforgettable for the exorbitant price being asked for a bottle of Coca-Cola in the terminal building;. The equivalent of one pound sterling was one hell of a lot of money in those days to pay for a fizzy drink. I think most of us stayed with either water or orange juice. I shudder to think what the price of a beer would have been. I recall a brief stop at RAF Khormaksar in Aden and the next port of call was El Adem. in Libya. On the ground there we were able to see Neville Duke's record breaking Hawker Hunter in which he had previously set a new world speed record flying at 727.63mph (1,171.01km/h). Not sure what that aircraft was doing at El Adem but I seem to remember talk of a possible attempt at another record. How true this was I have no idea.

Arriving back at Lynham in Wiltshire one very cold November evening we endured the usual scrutiny of our baggage and belongings by HM Customs and were then treated to a much needed meal. During the Customs inspection my pal John had his Hong Kong purchased watch confiscated as he was not able to afford the duty demanded of him. Later, whilst having our meal a Customs officer came into the dining hall, called out John's name and then returned his watch to him. I would imagine that a more senior and sympathetic officer had overruled the first chap's decision or the first fellow had suffered a pang of conscience. It may of course have been that the watch had been more closely examined and found to be not as valuable as at first thought.

By the time the formalities had been completed it was too late in the evening to head for our next destination No 5 PDU Lytham St Annes. We were then taken by bus to overnight accommodation at Clyffe Pypard a nearby former WWII airfield. Here we were billeted for the night in the usual style of wooden huts where most of us lost no time in getting to sleep. I don't think anyone was prepared for what was to greet us in the morning. The transport to convey us to the railway station in Swindon some seven miles (11kms) distant was scheduled to collect us quite early. With this in mind everyone, keen to be on their way left their beds sharply and went in search of the ablutions for a wash, shave and, if any were available a shower. What a shock, these facilities were outdoors in a flimsy structure open to the elements, showers were out of the question, it didn't look as if there were any. There were probably baths somewhere but after the first cold shock of the morning no one was keen to go looking for them. It was a case of stand and shiver whilst washing and shaving then retreat back inside the hut and don some warm clothing.

Why the formalities to get us on our way home for a spell of disembarkation leave could not have been handled at Lynham I have no idea. So it was off to Lytham St Annes for the second time in our career. No quick dip in the Irish Sea at Blackpool this time, not in November. I think we spent only one night at Lytham and once issued with rail warrants to take us home we were taken to the station. I do remember that a number of us enjoyed a farewell pint together whilst saying our goodbyes in the station buffet.

Upon successful completion of the Telegraphist 1 course the inevitable happened and I was posted outside the Y service to a hitherto, to me at least, unheard of Radar Station in the North-east of England, RAF Seaton Snook situated a few miles south of West Hartlepool. There I was the NCO i/c Station Signals which consisted of two single position telephone switchboards, one on the admin' site and one on the operations site some two miles distant where there was also a teleprinter. My staff were, one corporal telephonist who had until now quite easily handled this himself, six airman telephonists and one airman teleprinter operator. I really did have very little to do. The only reason for this 'overkill' to my mind is a cock-up at the RAF records office. The abbreviation for a Telegraphist was, at that time; Tel (either I or II), the abbreviation for Telephonist was simply Tel. It's entirely possible therefore that someone thought Seaton Snook needed two corporal telephonists and I was posted there in error as one of them. The SWO on this station was well-known for his loud voice. One day I was in the small telephone exchange in the Station Headquarters just a few doors away from the SWOs office. I just could not resist it when standing behind the lad operating the switchboard who answered a call from the SWO. I knew who was calling; I didn't need to be on line I could hear the SWOs loud voice through the open door. "Get me the Ops site" he shouted. Without waiting I said to the lad, "don't bother putting him through, I'll open the window, they'll hear him at Ops". "I heard that Corporal" screamed the SWO. He had of course heard me through the open line. To his credit he said no more, perhaps he saw the joke.

Although I had once been engaged to a girl in the North East I no longer had any personal ties in the region and I knew of a fellow ex-Boy Entrant stationed in the London area that was desirous of moving north, close to where his home was. We successfully arranged a swap, the service terminology for such procedure is known as an 'Exchange Posting. So, I then found myself as a corporal supervisor at the joint air traffic control centre at Hillingdon (Uxbridge) where life went on at a busy if a somewhat boring pace. I was, therefore, more than a little pleased one day, to receive a summons to attend an interview at RAF Wythall some 7 miles (11kms) south of Birmingham city centre to where the 'Y' School for the RAF had moved from Cheadle. Here I was asked if I was interested in going to Berlin with two other Corporals, yet to be selected, to replace three GCHQ civilians currently employed there. Was I interested? I certainly was, sitting in front of a radio receiver again was certainly preferable to supervising rows of airmen sitting at teleprinters day after day.

It was not uncommon in those days for Telegraphists and Wireless Operators employed in the Y service to find themselves posted to a non-Y Signals or Communications centre and once again be employed on the duties they had originally been trained for. This often placed such personnel in a difficult situation. They had, for a number of years been completely out of touch with procedures and systems in the world of telecommunications that was changing and advancing at a pace. They were, simply because they were qualified Telegraphists or Wireless Operators, expected to pick up the pieces and carry out their duties as though they had never been away. Such situations were the source of a certain amount of embarrassment, particularly for an NCO when he realised that airmen under his supervision knew more about the new systems and procedures than he did. It could also have a detrimental effect when he came to be assessed on his proficiency in the job. Thankfully for many, myself included this anomaly was eventually recognised and personnel employed in the Y service or having the appropriate qualifications were canvassed as to their preferences. The question asked was, if the trade were split, would they wish remain in the Y service and never again be employed on straight forward RAF Telecoms duties or would they wish to revert to their original trade? Whilst there were a small number of personnel that opted to revert, the majority, who had been working as intercept operators for a fair period of time, opted to stay with the Y service. Thus the new trade of Special Operator Telegraphy - Spec Op (T) was born. An adjunct to this was soon to be introduced, that of Special Operator

Voice - Spec Op (V) to accommodate linguists.

As I had been out of the Y service for a little over a year and in order for me to catch up on any recent developments or changes a refresher course at Wythall followed. As it happened, I was the only corporal in the class; the remainder were all SNCOs who had recently been recruited into the Y service. Following completion of this course and before the chosen three could set off to Berlin there was yet another course of training to undergo but more about that later.

3 THE COLD WAR AND A SUPER SPY

The RAF sigint facility in Berlin was, to begin with, staffed by a detachment of personnel from a major RAF sigint station in West Germany and a number of British Army Intelligence Corps personnel wearing the identification badges and flashes of the Royal Corps of Signals. This facility was located on RAF Station Gatow in south-western Berlin close to the small picturesque village of Kladow and the shores of the Havel river. I was to spend many a pleasant hour or so with my good friend and colleague Tony in the tiny bar and restaurant in Kladow enjoying a glass of *Schultheiss* beer or a *Berliner Weisse mit schütze.* Both enjoyable beverages even if the latter was more of a shandy, very refreshing on a hot summer's day. Tony and I would sometimes rent a small rowing boat to do a spot of fishing on the Havel. As I remember, we were never to catch anything but on one occasion Tony, not wanting to go home empty-handed paid a visit to the local fishmonger and bought some fish, not however of the species that we had been hoping to catch.

My involvement there together with Tony and another colleague was perhaps unique in the annals of service history. In the early 1950s one of the allotted tasks in what was at that time possibly the spy capital of Europe, was being performed by three civilian ROs (Radio Officers) from GCHQ. Their job was to search the short-wave radio bands for, listen to and transcribe details of Soviet Diplomatic and Illicit Morse transmissions.

Such transmissions originated mainly in Moscow or in Soviet embassies and Consuls in the Eastern Block. These transmissions in Morse code were always, at that time hand-sent as opposed to some traffic these days that employs a pre-prepared tape via a machine or another electronic device. The messages, from the 'agents' however, when one was fortunate enough to intercept such, were usually sent using a device linked to the transmitter that resulted in the message being sent at very high-speed. This device is known as a 'burst' transmitter of which more shortly.

The diplomatic traffic would of course have been to their embassies or consuls in the west but that which was tagged Illicit would have been transmissions direct to or from Soviet or East German agents, the Krogers sentenced to twenty years each for spying in 1961 among them. Readers of tales of Cold War espionage will be familiar with the activities of Peter and Helen Kroger, real names Morris and Leontina (known as Lona or Lena) Cohen, an American Jewish couple. They lived comfortably in a semi-detached house in a respectable West London suburb and had a fairly extensive quantity of espionage paraphernalia including an instrument known as a 'Burst' Transmitter. It in itself is not a transmitter but an encoder connected to the transmitter. There were and still are many variations of this device upon which a message is stored on a variety of mediums such as photographic film, audio, metal or paper tape with the message typed upon it. The prepared medium is then fed into the encoder linked to the transmitter resulting in it being transmitted in very high speed Morse code, 200 - 250 wpm (words per minute). A most desirable piece of equipment for any agent to transmit their reports to their masters at speed.

As all radio transmissions are capable of being intercepted the speed of transmission was, and indeed still is, essential. Employing a normal radio transmitter to send a message by hand using a Morse key, even one designed to enable one to speed up the sending, would mean the agent being on the air long enough for the intercepting station to ascertain the location of the transmitter by one or more direction finding stations. Using three such DF stations to triangulate the signal would result in a very accurate result, known as a 'fix'. However, using this 'burst' facility linked to a transmitter the time on the air would be reduced to anything from a few seconds to not much more than 15-20 seconds at the most leaving little or no time at all for details to be passed to DF stations and for a bearing to be taken. Where the 'Burst' transmission failed however was, prior to the actual start of the message there was always a steady and rapid stream of dots. The intercept operator would initially be listening to the control and would have no idea of the frequency upon which the agent would send his traffic. However, should the control be expecting a message he, having previously requested the agent to obtain certain information, would send a five figure group, usually all the same figures, e.g. 33333 as an indicator to the agent to go ahead and send his traffic. It was at this stage that the intercepting operator would start a hurried search on his second radio receiver. If this search found the frequency quickly enough, he would hear the stream of dots, referred to as 'Revs' and be able to feed the frequency to a DF station. These were the type of transmissions that the 'three' in Berlin were so keen to intercept. The control always had a very strong signal, sometimes so strong that we often joked about the possibility of the transmitter being in the RAF station's boiler house a short distance away down the road. It is more than likely however, that most Control transmissions originated in East Berlin or Moscow. The intercepted messages, be they in either Morse or voice, were always in the form of what is now referred to as 'numbers', five figure groups of numbers in messages of varying length preceded in this case, by a three figure call-sign. I believe the encryption method was of the one-time-pad type and this is borne out by subsequent arrests of agents complete with their paraphernalia including their one-time pads. The equipment in use on two desks was the ubiquitous HRO, two, mounted one above the other, a large Ferrograph reel-to-reel tape recorder and a field telephone connected to the DF site on the airfield.

In common with all other British Intelligence staff in Berlin, the administration facilities for the three civilian ROs were located in the Olympic stadium, the Headquarters SIS (Secret Intelligence Service - MI6) in Berlin but their place of work was in a small office on Royal Air Force station Gatow. One can only suppose that this location was selected because listening facilities in the form of antennae were already in place or could be made readily available. This office was on the second floor of SHQ (Station Headquarters) to start with and in order to reach it one had to ascend a flight of stairs upon which, midway, was a checkpoint manned by an armed guard from the RAF

Regiment. Access past this point would only be permitted upon proof of identity and entitlement to be in such a place. On the same floor and along a corridor, a number of RAF and Army linguists were at work eavesdropping on Soviet military communications and similar transmissions of other Warsaw Pact nations.

Sometime in the early 1950s, GCHQ decided to withdraw these three civilians and replace them with three cut-price operators, three RAF NCOs (Non-Commissioned Officers). One can only speculate the reasons for this. It may well have been down to budgetary constraints. It seems that in the 1950s requests to the treasury by GCHQ and its sister organisations MI5 and MI6 for funding were not favourably received. With this in mind, these secret service organisations were most likely, always looking for ways to cut costs without reducing the efficiency of their operations. True enough, the three civilian ROs were well paid and in receipt of an extra overseas allowance but the cost of housing them and their families who accompanied them would have been minimal. They were accommodated in an apartment complex in the Charlottenburg area of Berlin a fairly select suburb. This allocated accommodation had been requisitioned by the British government to house such personnel including SIS and other officials. The apartments were there and it mattered not whether they were occupied or otherwise. The only on-going expense would have been the cost of maintenance. The real reason that the three civilian operators were being replaced may of course had nothing whatsoever to do with security or budgetary constraints. It may simply have been that they were not producing the results that GCHQ expected of them. It is entirely possible that on occasions other stations in Europe although not tasked with that particular job, had intercepted, on a casual basis, some of the traffic that the three should also have logged but had not. If this was so it would have raised questions in the minds of the analysts at GCHQ leading to a decision to replace the present incumbents.

In Peter Wright's *Spycatcher* [14] he refers to the "Paltry one and half positions" allotted to the task in hand, meaning that three operators covering a 24 hour period was a long way short of being enough when periods of leave or sickness were taken into account. Peter Wright also stated that he wanted GCHQ to provide a better service devoted to monitoring 'Illegal' Soviet radio broadcasts but it seems that no amount of persuasion could make them provide anything more than this, at least in the short term. The obvious cost cutting solution would be to replace the three civilian ROs with three 'bargain basement' armed forces operators and, as the location for this particular operation was on an RAF Base, then the obvious choice would be three experienced RAF Special Operators. Whilst this solution did not respond to Peter Wright's requests one could assume that it would go some way to perhaps showing the Treasury that they were making an effort to keep their finances in order and stand them in good stead the next time they sought some extra funding. In addition, the Service-for-Civilian replacement would solve a security problem that had probably not even been thought about. Here we had three chaps in civilian attire, and known to be regular visitors to their parent offices of administration in the Olympic stadium, with one or more of them visiting an RAF Station at various hours of the day or night, but for what reason? Any spy worth his salt would certainly have thought that such activity was worth investigating. Such movements would certainly have been known to any mole employed in, and operating out of the stadium and there was a very infamous one in situ, as we shall see. This was Berlin after all, the movements of these three ROs, together with most, if not all incumbents of the stadium offices were probably already well monitored by other sources or 'watchers'. So, replace them with three uniformed airmen who lived on the station anyway, nothing unusual in that at all so no suspicions would be aroused.

Before setting off for Berlin and at the request, or rather the demand, of GCHQ the three specially selected RAF Junior NCOs of which I was one, were detailed to attend the civilian Radio Officers course at CTS (Central Training School) Bletchley Park. This was to be my second visit to the now famously known Station X. On my first visit to undergo a short specialist course, a couple of us managed to blot our copybooks whilst indulging in a little lunchtime sport. It didn't take us long to discover that there were a good number of fish in the large EWS (Emergency Water Supply) tank close to the main building. Makeshift rods were soon manufactured from bits of stick, strong twine and bent pins and it was off for a spot of angling during the lunch hour. Our relaxation was however, short-lived. Someone must have ratted on us to the Admin' lady and she came screaming out of her office, gave us a right mouthful, demanded to know who we were (we all wore civilian clothes at Bletchley Park) and said she would report us. As we heard no more of the incident I can only assume that someone either had a sense of humour or considered that our lunchtime entertainment was not likely to be repeated seeing as we had been verbally whip-lashed by Madam Admin.

Leaving aside the fun part of being at Bletchley Park the course we attended on this first visit was the civilian Radio Operators General Search (GS) course. As readers will have seen, I have already made reference to GS during the previous chapter on Hong Kong. This particular course at Bletchley Park was more concerned with foreign transmissions that an operator was likely to encounter during his service in Europe. For the six weeks that the course lasted one spent each day listening to extracts of transmissions in Morse from a myriad of countries. Such extracts consisted mainly of call up patterns and message preambles in use. As an example, most European military stations, when one was calling another, would use *'de'* (the French for from). ABC *de* GEF would tell the intercepting operator that station GEF was calling station ABC. However, one other service in Europe, I am no longer sure which after all this time but it may have been Italian Naval or Police authorities who would use 'vvv' instead of 'de'. British military at that time would use 'v' instead of 'de' and so on. Such differences in procedures were an immediate aid to recognition of the station one was hearing. Considering that most stations used *'de'* in the call up further recognition did not always come that easy but there were also a number of 'giveaways' in procedures. After such a long time, more than sixty years ago in fact, it is difficult to remember most of them but one that sticks in my mind was the use of *'Niet Geheim'* (Non-Secret)in the preamble of an intercepted message. This would tell us that the message about to be transmitted was practice or exercise traffic emanating from a Dutch military station. These are just a few of the examples of the information that one needed to retain to enable one to become an efficient GS operator. The examination at the end of the course consisted of being given twenty-two log sheets, each containing an extract from intercepted foreign signals traffic and one had to correctly identify as many as possible, not only to the country but also to the particular service of origin. Not a difficult task if one had taken in all one was being taught. I found the course really interesting in that it gave one an insight into the various telecommunications procedures of countries other than those normally being targeted during the Cold War. I must stress here that the purpose of being able to recognise allied or friendly nations signals traffic was not with the intention of analysing or using it in any way. Knowledge of such transmissions and recognising the country of origin enabled the operator to 'drop' or leave that particular intercept and press on searching for transmissions of 'target' nations.

My second visit, considered necessary by GCHQ to ensure that we three were up to the standard required to replace three of their operators was of a longer duration but equally enjoyable even though quite intense. For a number of consecutive days one had to take a Morse test of fifteen minutes duration that consisted of three parts. One part was all foreign plain text, the second part consisted of groups of five letters including Cyrillic and the final part being groups of five letters and figures mixed that went under the name of Cyco. This test at 25wpm not only had to be passed on three consecutive days without error but also once passed the student had to convince the examiner that all that he had written was perfectly legible, also over a period of three days. Another part of the course involved Morse Slip reading at speed, usually about 45wpm. This was the practice of transcribing on to a typewriter Morse symbols printed as short and slightly longer lines representing the dots and dashes, by a machine known as an undulator onto an absorbent paper tape. Apparently this was something in use at Bletchley Park during WWII but I never saw it in use anywhere during my time in the Y service. We also spent a good deal of our time on the course intercepting what was known as 'synthetic' transmissions. These were transmissions resembling foreign signals traffic composed and fed by the instructional staff into receivers at which we would sit. Usually two separate stations would be heard working together, each on a different frequency so one had two receivers with which to jiggle. All fine until one station instructed the other to change frequency and one had to frantically search on one receiver for the new frequency. Having found the new frequency the station would sometimes 'hop' to another. The instructional staff at Bletchley were rather hot on this and didn't always give one much time to execute this procedure. An exercise that required all ones undivided attention but one that had its benefits later on when having to perform such procedures in the field as it were. Some time was also spent in a large room that contained a wide variety of radio receivers of varying vintage, many of them that remained from WWII. This was a most interesting place as one got to experience tuning and twiddling the dials and controls of equipment that one was unlikely ever to see again. That is of course unless one was an enthusiast or collector of vintage radio equipment and there are such folk. An enjoyable hobby I should think having seen and enjoyed using, albeit for a short time just what can still be found out there.

With this second course completed and kit packed it was off to Berlin via RAF Innsworth (Gloucestershire), Harwich and the Hook of Holland, or so we thought. After a few nights in a transit camp at Goch just over the Dutch border into Germany we arrived at RAF Station Scharfoldendorf in the Hartz Mountains region. In Hitler's Germany Scharfoldendorf was the location of *Gruppe 9* of the *NSFK (Nationalsozialistisches Fliegerkorps)* [15] part of the Hitler *Jungend* or Hitler Youth organisation. This was, following the end of war, to become a German civilian gliding club based to the rear of the camp and very active during my short stay there. No one seemed to know what we were doing there, and as far as the administrators were concerned we should have been in Berlin. We were given accommodation in a very nice block with all mod cons and told to check daily with the Orderly Room and then left to our own devices. Who were we to turn down a holiday in this beautiful part of the globe? The nearest town of any note was Hameln to which we made a visit or two. One of the three of us, Tony, who had already previously served in the area, knew Hameln well and was able to show us the bars and other places of interest. Here I was treading the streets of the legendary *Rattenfänger von Hameln* or the Pied Piper of Hamelin as most of us know him from the Grimm Brothers tales we were to read or that were read to us in our childhood. It is impossible to visit Hamelin without seeing reminders of this medieval fairy tale that is re-enacted in the town on Sundays during the summer months.

One particularly sunny Saturday afternoon I took myself off for a walk over the surrounding hills. Climbing up a steep rise out of some woodland I was attracted by a strange whirring noise from above. Looking up I saw, about 2000 feet (600 metres) above the ground, a stationary glider that appeared to vibrate frantically before plunging earthwards. I didn't see, but did hear, its contact with the ground as it disappeared into a small hollow a little further up the hill. Hurrying up there and looking down all I could see was what looked like a great pile of matchwood spread over a small area. In the centre of this debris lay what was clearly a body clothed in a dark green pullover and dark trousers. I was soon to be joined by a number of people who had come running over the hill from the launch site. The following day I was to learn that the poor unfortunate glider pilot had apparently suffered a heart attack whilst in the air. This unhappy incident shook me up to the extent that I have, since that day, had to decline any offers I have received to take a flight in a glider.

Our next routine visit to the Orderly Room, the office where all the stations administration is dealt with, or should be, revealed that we were not now to head further east but to return to the UK. GCHQ had stepped in by requesting, or rather insisting that we return to Cheltenham for a briefing on what we were expected to do in Berlin. A week was then spent in transit at RAF Innsworth. We were given instructions on how to get to GCHQ by using public transport and told that the bus stopped right outside the gate of the Ministry of Pensions. The bus did indeed stop there and somewhat bewildered this is where we alighted. The sign opposite the bus stop announced that we had arrived at the aforementioned ministry but there was no indication as to the location of GCHQ. Now the whole world knows where it is and what goes on there. No doubt the Ministry of Pensions sign has long since been removed.

Once inside the precincts of this holy of holy we were met and guided by an RAF Secretarial Branch Sergeant, a Dubliner who had a fund of jokes to tell, all clean and mostly corny. 'Paddy' wasn't allowed into the inner sanctum, he was merely there to liaise with the likes of ourselves and ensure that we were fed and watered. Soon after our arrival on site he was to escort us to the point where we were issued with passes to the 'inside'.

We were given a through briefing on what was expected of us in Berlin, how the results of our work was to be despatched and received by themselves and the general picture of the Berlin situation to date. In addition, we were also instructed exactly as to where in those buildings our passes would allow us to wander. As we needed only to visit two of the offices we couldn't wander very far, a 'need to know' principle was strictly enforced. We didn't however feel ostracised or 'left out' by these restrictions as we soon came to realise that there were many permanent staff there that were denied access to the two rooms in which we were being briefed. Once everyone was satisfied that these three Air Force types were not going to make a hash of things we were, after spending a week-end at home, free finally to make our way direct to Berlin. This journey once again via Harwich and the Hook of Holland but this time missing out Scharfholdendorf where the efforts of some wag there appending an unofficial addition to the notices on SROs still make me smile.

Less than half a mile to the rear of the station, the other side of the gliding club in fact, there was a DP (Displaced Persons) camp. The inhabitants of this camp were believed to be refugees from Eastern Europe and some were, quite possibly 'plants' sent there to become agents when finally established in the West. A notice regularly posted on SROs reminded all personnel that the nearby DP camp was out of bounds and they were not, under any circumstances to visit the place. In those days all RAF personnel stationed in Germany received their pay in BAFVS, (British Armed Forces Vouchers). These vouchers were legal tender only in the NAAFI and other similar facilities on the station. Should anyone want to shop or visit bars and restaurants outside the camp and everyone did, then they had to exchange their vouchers for West German Marks. To enable such exchange to take place there was a facility, usually in the accounts section of the station and the time when such a convenience would be available was always published in SROs. On this occasion the notice, printed beneath the DP camp reminder, reading something like, BAFVS/Deutsch Marks exchange facility will be available in the Accounts section on Thursday between 1400 and 1600 hours. Beneath this notice some wag had neatly written "Roubles exchange to take place immediately afterwards". I never heard of anyone being disciplined for defacing SROs, and I don't think any action was taken on this occasion.

As most readers will be well aware, Germany, at the end of WWII was divided up into Zones between the four occupying powers, The Soviet Union taking a third of the country in the east and the other three powers, America, France and Great Britain occupying the remaining two thirds in the west. As a result, Berlin became a virtual island in the Soviet Zone and was similarly divided up into four Sectors.

The journey to Berlin was by Military Train operated by the British Army's Royal Corps of Transport and departing each night from Hanover, to begin its journey through the Soviet Zone to Charlotenburg in West Berlin where it arrived early the next morning. Once on board the train ones identity documents were collected up and handed to the train Sergeant Major who would retain them until its first and only stopping point on the journey, Helmstedt/Marienborn checkpoint on the East German border. At this checkpoint the identity documents held by the Sergeant Major would be checked by a Soviet Officer and if he was satisfied then the train was allowed to continue on its way. I seem to remember decent meals being served on board by pleasant German female staff.

Shortly after arriving in Berlin and settling in to our allotted accommodation we were given a comprehensive handover by the outgoing ROs. This handover was not all work however, it included sightseeing trips around Berlin and a visit to some of the nightspots. One highlight being a visit to a basement bar known as 26 Mess. This was not open to the public but was a club for, and frequented by, the British intelligence community. Above the stairs leading down to the bar in the basement was a large shield featuring a cloak and dagger figure, not unlike the cloaked figure in the Sandeman sherry advert' but this one sporting a dagger in addition to the cloak. It was in the bar here that a well-built fellow, with beard and known to all as 'The Dutchman' was pointed out to the three new arrivals. What I did not realise until some years later was that the 'Dutchman' was in fact George Blake, possibly one of the most infamous spies of the Twentieth century! The very chap who was soon to reveal to his Soviet masters the secrets of the tunnel. This was a tunnel built by the Americans and equipped with electronic monitoring devices. It was about 500 yards in length and went from a suburb in the American Sector to a suburb in East Berlin in the Soviet Sector. The sole purpose of this tunnel being to house the equipment needed to intercept and record telephone traffic including Soviet communications, emanating from East Berlin. And this was the 'Dutchman' that worked out of the offices in the Berlin Olympic Stadium and where no doubt he obtained much of his intelligence to pass on to the Soviets.

This and many other traitorous exploits including allegedly passing information to his contacts about personalities who had defected from the east, subsequently resulting in their kidnapping and execution, are well documented and published in book form. Montgomery Hyde's book, *George Blake Super Spy* [16] is a fascinating account of the life of a spy. George Blake, sentenced to 42 years imprisonment in 1961, escaped from Wormwood Scrubs in 1966 aided by Seán Bourke, an Irishman and fellow prisoner of Blake. Details of this daring and somewhat ingenious escape are well detailed in Seán Bourke's book *The Springing of George Blake*. [17] Seán Bourke himself spent a short time in the RAF but was dishonourably discharged for alleged theft.[18] He, not surprisingly, made no mention of this in his book which incidentally I found to be an excellent read covering not only details of the escape but of the two fascinating years that Bourke himself spent in Russia prior to returning to Ireland in 1968. The copy I have was published by the Literary Guild London by arrangement with Cassell and contains a very good fold out map of the area around Wormwood Scrubs. Seán Bourke died in his home town in County Clare in January 1982.

An added perk, if one can call it a perk, for the three RAF NCOs was the entire absence of any requirement whatsoever to carry out any extraneous duties whilst at Gatow. Parades, ceremonial or otherwise were also avoided. The reason for this exemption being that the hours of duty in the office were, in part, often dictated by the intercepted traffic. A message intercepted at, for example, 1500 hours could indicate that further traffic was scheduled for 0200 hours the next morning. The manner in which we obtained the details of the forecast transmission schedule was not by deciphering the message, we were not able to do this as such traffic was undoubtedly enciphered by the one-time pad [19] method (OTP) and not breakable or decipherable. Fortunately for us however, the last two groups of the message were decipherable simply by subtracting the day and date from them. This would then give one the time and date of the Control's next transmission. Very helpful indeed but I should think this simple 'give away' is no longer in use by any of today's participants involved in transmitting Diplomatic or Illicit traffic over the short waves.

Of course not all hours worked were dictated by the schedules, during the day at least two of these three merry men would be at work in the office searching the airwaves for more Diplomatic or Illicit Morse code traffic and if lucky, schedules to be followed up. The Soviets did not however, always play fairly. Early on in our tour of duty, one of the controls decided to switch from Morse to Voice. As far as we were aware this trick had not been used when the GCHQ civilians were in situ. Reacting to this unfortunate switch in tactics one of our number dashed down the corridor to our Russian linguist colleagues and had them write down phonetically, the numbers zero to nine in Russian. We were quick to learn these off pat and return to situation normal.

The hours of work were unsociable and not hours that anyone else on the station would be required to work. However, this was not without certain advantages. Sometimes being in the office late at night or in the early hours and intercepting traffic that indicated nothing further would be transmitted from a particular source until later that day meant that, if one felt inclined, one could sign off, nip down in to Berlin to Dicker Heinrich's (Fat Henry's). This was a bar specialising in roast or grilled chicken, where one could enjoy a beer and half a roast chicken before returning home and retiring to bed. On one visit there Fat Henry asked me if I was a doctor. There did not seem to be an emergency at the time and I never did find out why such a question was asked.

Opposite our room in SHQ there was another small room that as far as we were ever able to see, contained a bed and not much else. The only person who ever seemed to occupy this room was a mysterious gent in civilian clothing who would always arrive at the dead of night lugging what appeared to be a heavy suitcase from which, on occasion, loud 'clanging' noises were heard. This fellow never spoke to anyone or acknowledged any greeting and was always very careful to lock the door behind him once he entered his room. After a while it became a bit of a game as this chap, having no idea who he was, we referred to him as the Queens Messenger, would often try to have a peek into our domain whilst opening his door. Whoever was on watch at the time would then very pointedly close our door to preventing him seeing in. Daft maybe but it was a case of tit for tat, he wouldn't let us see into his place so no way was he going to see into ours! This 'messenger' would depart from Gatow on the regular RAF flight to RAF Northholt in South Ruislip in the London Borough of Hillingdon. He never used the passenger terminal but was picked up by a Corporal driver in a Volkswagen Beetle and taken to board the aircraft on the taxiway.

This corporal driver was also something of a mystery. He did not seem to belong to the MT section on the station and never drove anything or anyone else. We often spoke with him and he told us he was attached to the station from 'down the zone'. Since that time however, with so much of what was formerly 'sensitive' information entering the public domain I think it is fair to assume that the mysterious gent and his driver were from BRIXMIS (The British Commander in Chiefs Mission to the Soviet Forces in Germany). BRIXMIS was the very successful British Intelligence gathering organisation operating out of Berlin and into the Soviet Zone of Germany consisting of personnel from all three services and a few civilians with temporary local Army ranks. They were also known to 'collect' certain items of interest that were sent back to the UK for examination and analysis. I now believe that some of such items possibly made up the contents of the suitcase carried by the mysterious gent when he locked himself in his room whilst awaiting the next RAF flight out of Berlin.

Off duty I was still playing rugby at least once per week in the season. I must have been far from the best player in the team as when the Berlin Rugby Club were our opponents and were a number of players short I and one other were 'loaned' to them. At least I can say that I played Rugby for Berlin! Shortly after this I suffered a back injury whilst playing and ended up in hospital for a number of weeks followed by a long period of physiotherapy. The physiotherapist was a very attractive Hungarian lady and a most capable masseuse. I must confess to having enjoyed my visits to the hospital for this treatment. I was to meet this lady some months later on a visit to the hospital and she questioned me as to why I was no longer going for treatment. She seemed as disappointed as was I although I was pleased to no longer have the back problem. The British Military Hospital (BMH) in Berlin was located in the district of Spandau and in the time I spent there I was in a small ward with three or four soldiers. Two of these soldiers had recently completed a spell of duty on guard at Spandau Jail in which the prisoners at that time were the infamous Rudolf Hess, Grand Admiral Karl Dönitz, Baldur von Schirach and Albert Speer. Dönitz was released on 1st October 1956, during my time there, Von Schirach, Head of the Hitler Youth, in September 1966 and Albert Speer, Minister of Armaments and War Production on 1st October 1966. Hess remained the solitary prisoner there until death by his own hand, on 17th August 1987 aged 93. The manner of his death is disputed by some who claim that he was murdered by the British Secret Service.

In addition to playing rugby I also found time to learn to sail on the Havel, part of the large inland lake/river complex that includes Lake Wansee. These lakes were accessible not only from the British Sector, in our case within walking distance of RAF Gatow but also from the American and Soviet sectors of Berlin and to The French sector via a series of smaller channels. Before I was allowed to take a small Olympic class sailing dinghy out alone I had to pass a test to assess my performance and capabilities in an emergency. I was, on this occasion very privileged to have as my examiner one Major Chris Hallet MBE MC of BRIXMIS, a brave and courageous officer with a string of cold war Technical Intelligence coups to his name [20]. I feel honoured to have spent some time in his company. I also enjoyed sailing as crew on 'Wannsee' (named after the lake) a Star Class yacht that in the 1936 Olympic Games was the winner in its class for Germany. All the yachts in the British Berlin Yacht Club were former German owned and were seized as reparations in 1945 at the end of the Second World War.

One of my very good friends in Berlin, Fred, a Corporal in the station's MT (Motor Transport) section owned a very nice, nearly new car, an Opel Record. At this time such vehicles were not available in the UK. Opel, being part of the General Motors Group their vehicles manufactured in Germany would have been in direct opposition to Vauxhall products in the UK. Conversely Vauxhall cars were not sold in Germany for similar reasons. Fred was about to come to the end of his tour in Berlin and offered to sell me this car at a very reasonable price. I was happy to do this but first, never having owned a car before I had first to learn to drive! As luck would have it the same MT section also had a driving school, the pupils being in the main, from other units or sections on the station where their commanding officer had decided that it would be advantageous for them to learn to drive. My CO who was really only a figurehead as far as I was concerned, was not aware and was not told the purpose of my being there. All he knew was that I, along with my two colleagues, worked strange hours and the product of our work ended up at GCHQ via the daily Diplomatic Bag from Templehof airport. He really he had no valid reason for recommending that I learn to drive. Fortunately, my friend Fred had a good working relationship with the sergeant in charge of the MT section who was also the driving examiner and he was persuaded to take me on as a pupil in the driving school. Lessons were for two to three hours twice per week and consisted of initially driving around the roads in the Berlin Grunewald Forest and often close to the shores of Lake Wannsse where the roads were quiet, sometimes in convoy with other vehicles. It was here at a villa on the shores of Lake Wannsee in January 1942 that the 'Final Solution' to the Jewish question was discussed and the methods used to implement same decided upon. [21] Chairing the meeting that resulted in the mass murder of six million people was Reinhard Heydrich who was assisted by another infamous Nazi, Adolf Eichmann. The rest of this murderous group was made up of top Nazi officials from various ministries and from the Gestapo and other security agencies. Myself and possibly all the other trainee drivers were certainly not, at this time, aware that such a notorious event had taken place so close to where we were then enjoying a drive around the now peaceful lanes of a most attractive and affluent Berlin suburb. Another interesting feature close by is the *Glienicker Brücke* or Glienicker Bridge that spans the Havel River. During the Cold War this bridge was a restricted border crossing between the Soviet and American sectors of Berlin and was used to facilitate the exchange of spies between East and West. During my time in Berlin this was yet to happen as the first exchange took place in 1962 when the Americans swapped the Soviet spy Rudolf Abel for Gary Powers the U-2 spy plane pilot, shot-down by the Soviets in 1960.[22] A number of other spy exchanges were to follow leading to the bridge being referred to in the media as 'The Bridge of Spies'.

When one became competent and more sure of oneself behind the wheel most of the lessons took place within the city of Berlin itself. The vehicles used were large Magirus Deutz 3.5-Ton trucks. No such thing as synchromesh gears in those days, not on heavy vehicles at least. In order to change gear one had to double de-clutch, a movement that did not always come easy to many but once mastered became second nature. I think many of today's younger drivers being used to the luxury of present day vehicles would find this procedure rather irksome. At one stage my instructor, a very able SAC (Senior Aircraftman) MT driver by trade, when we were not in convoy, decided that a spin round the Avus,[23] a pre-war motor racing circuit, would be nice. The Avus was originally an experimental motorway upon which construction started prior to WWI but was halted and work did not recommence until after the end of that conflict. It's construction was such that it could also be used as a motor racing circuit and the first race there took place in 1921. It was indeed fun, the track having a loop at one end, sort of basin shaped so at all times on this part of the circuit we were approaching an angle of 43°, OK in a normal passenger car or a Formula 1 racing car, in a 3.5-Ton truck it was something else. Sadly the Avus was closed in 1999 and is no more, well not as either a motorway or a racing circuit. Following its sale to a developer some of the buildings including the race control tower were converted into a motel and restaurant.

Came the day of reckoning, the time to take my test. Surprise, surprise, reporting to the sergeant examiner at the MT section he indicated that I climb into the Magirus. Since the last time I drove this vehicle, just a couple of days previous, it had grown somewhat. There was now a huge snowplough attached to its front end. Ah well, thought I, at least people should get out of my way in the city now, making my life easier. Driving around Berlin I suppose is not a lot different from to doing the same in any other large and busy city including those, like Berlin, that have trams in the middle of the road. In the busy area to which we were destined on that day the roads were not particularly wide which gave one the impression that the tram was taking up more than its fair share of the highway. My instructor however, had given me a good deal of practice approaching tram stops. When a tram stops in Berlin alighting passengers have priority over any adjacent traffic so one must stop to allow them free passage to safety. It was a busy day in Spandau, this being the part of the city where most of the test took place. Thankfully I negotiated the district without incident although I must say I did perform a few rapid stopping movements when the occasional tram came to a stop when I was not expecting it. All went well and I was directed to return to the MT section at RAF Gatow. Arriving there and vacating the Magirus, the examining sergeant duly scanning his clip board on which he had been making notes throughout the journey, looked at me and said, "OK you've passed that bit now get in that", pointing at, after what I had just experienced, something that looked like a toy car, a Volkswagen Beetle. The day was turning out to be full of surprises. Seeing the look of surprise on my face he said something to the effect that I was fine in the Magi' but lets see what you can do in the VW, after all you will be expected to drive both. No one, not even Fred had told me about this, all sorts of thoughts were going through my mind, are the controls the same? Do I still have to double de-clutch etc? As luck would have it I had little to worry about once I had journeyed down the road for a few kilometres, everything was more or less in the same place, just smaller. I did double de-clutch whether I needed to or not, and the sergeant seemed impressed. My only problem was keeping the speed down now that I was in a vehicle that answered somewhat more sharply to the pedal but after a couple of sharp reminders from my examiner I soon got the hang of it. Following a few circuits of Spandau we returned to base where I was happy to be told I had passed and was pleased to receive the form that when completed would get me, in addition to an official RAF driving permit (Form 1629), my British Forces Germany driving licence. The RAF licence would, if I had been an RAF driver by trade, enable me to obtain, when produced in the UK, together with another document, a full civilian UK licence. Unfortunately as this was not my calling, should I want to drive on the UK roads on my eventual return I would, as does everyone else, have to take the UK test.

As with so many other enjoyable and happy incidents in life, all good things must come to an end. The three of us did apply for an extension of tour, the normal RAF overseas tour being one of two and a half years duration, but this was refused, possibly someone in a seat of power thought we were enjoying ourselves too much!

So, now it was time to plan the journey home. How much simpler in those days it was to import left-hand drive vehicle into the UK. All I needed to do to smooth the passage by having most things organised for me was to join the AA (Automobile Association) as an overseas member and then arrive at Dover via one of the European channel ports and they would take care of any legalities. As the number plates on the car identified it as a British Zone of Germany registered vehicle, V108BZ, these plates would have to be changed. Having forwarded my details to the AA together with a UK address I received the notification that my car was now registered in the UK with the number VGJ 55. In addition I was informed that I could, on arrival in Dover, collect my new plates from the AA office there although I would not need to change them until I reached my destination to which I would lawfully be permitted to drive. I would also be permitted to continue to drive said vehicle in the UK provided I attached a small black patch to an appropriate position on the headlights ensuring that I would not now dazzle oncoming drivers with my headlights now dipping the wrong way. All that remained would be my need to obtain a full UK driving licence, which I did after taking a test in Royal Leamington Spa, a charming little town. These days apparently, should I be importing a similar vehicle into the UK I would need to attend a special centre of which I believe there are a number throughout the country, for it to undergo an examination to certify that it conformed to the standards required for use on UK roads. No little black patch on the headlights either, they would have to be completely changed. Oh how complicated life has become since then, I don't suppose we realised in the 50s just how lucky we were to be living in such easygoing uncomplicated times.

That part of the journey as one can see was straight forward, not so the pantomime involved to enable one to finally depart Berlin, not for indoctrinated personnel in the Y service anyway as it involved a three hour drive through East Germany or the DDR as the communist authorities preferred it to be known. Should I have been cook, an MT driver, a Supplier (storeman) or some such trade that needed no indoctrination then it would have been simple, I would have been issued with the necessary document, in both English and Russian and this together with proof of my identity would have been sufficient to get me through the Soviet check-point on the Autobahn. It would seem however, that personnel in the Y service held too many secrets in their heads and would therefore need to be de-indoctrinated or, as we would say, 'brainwashed'. In order for this to happen one had to journey to

Scharfoldendorf in West Germany either by civil aircraft or by the military train to Hanover, thence onward by RAF transport, for the purpose of signing a document. This document was simply a declaration that one was agreeing not, during the next five years, to visit any of the communist countries listed including Cuba. Document duly signed one then retraced ones steps back to Berlin, almost always by the military train on this return journey. Back at RAF Gatow it was no longer possible to enter the secure area where one had previously been employed. Having been de-indoctrinated one no longer had any secrets in the head and this restriction would prevent one having further access to any, at least that is, not until arriving safely in the West, crazy! I have never understood why this journey had to be made and any such de-indoctrination procedures could not have taken place in Berlin but as the saying goes, "Ours is not to reason why, ours is but to do or die"

Within a few short days of being 'brainwashed' and returning to Gatow it was a case of bags packed, the necessary documents obtained and set off on the journey by car to the channel port of ones choice via East then West Germany, Holland, Belgium and France. The journey itself was fairly uneventful and having handed in my identity documents at the Marienborne/Helmstedt checkpoint for the Soviet military to examine and no doubt photocopy I was able and happy to continue my journey through to West Germany and beyond. We made a night stop at Aachen on the Dutch border where I experienced for the first time sleeping beneath a duvet or, as the Germans would say a *Federbett* (feather bed). I am well aware that duvets and feather beds are now common place but in the UK in those days they were not, how things have changed for the better in that department. Belgium could have been missed out but I was travelling in tandem with my friend and colleague Tony who was having problems with his vehicle. This was an ageing Standard Vanguard and I was there as a back-up in case he needed assistance. Tony was sailing from Ostend to Harwich so we had a pleasant meal together in the port of Ostend before I set off for Calais. I was aware that I would need to produce certain documents at the Belgium/France border crossing so I decided to check these before finally setting of on this, the final stage of my European mainland journey. One of the documents that I had previously been informed I would need at the French border crossing related to the vehicle and concerned ones allocation of a monthly ration of duty-free petrol from the filling stations in Berlin among other things. When I took this document out of my small document case I was more than a little surprised to see that it related to a Porsche, not to my Opel Record. This document had been handed to me by the officer responsible for the updating of such documents and at the time he presented it to me he had obviously enjoyed his, possibly liquid, lunch in the Officers Mess. This officer was well known to me as a fellow member of the station Rugby team so we spent a pleasant 20 minutes or so chatting whilst I tucked the document away with the others I needed for the journey. My problem now was, what do I do at the French border now that I no longer had one of the documents needed. In the end I just decided to bluff it out and produce another document that contained details of the vehicle. I no longer remember which one, it may have been the logbook. Handing this over to the solitary uniformed official on duty with what I thought would pass for a friendly smile I held my breath. This elderly chap gave my documents, including the substitute one, only a perfunctory glance before handing them back to me and wishing me *Bon Voyage*. I exited the office with a feeling of great relief, for a moment it had shades of a flashback to the time when, not so long ago, France was under Nazi occupation and so many brave good folk travelled around on false documents. I was almost beginning to know how those folk must have felt. I did wonder what the reaction of the owner of the Porsche must have been when either he did not receive his document back following its update or he received one relating to an Opel Record. I returned his document to Berlin by post shortly after arriving in the UK in the hope that it would soon be reunited with its owner.

The trip through East Germany or the DDR was not always so smooth for everyone. Some years later whilst in Singapore I was to meet an RAF Regiment sergeant who I had been acquainted with in

Berlin. He apparently did not have an easy trip after departing Berlin where he was, at one stage, whilst still in the Soviet Zone run off the road by a couple of guys on motor bikes. He sat abandoned for about half-an-hour when a *VoPo (Volkspolizei,* East German Police) patrol turned up and offered to get him back on the road. He refused their offer by sticking to the standard briefing. Prior to leaving Gatow he would have been informed, in writing, that should he get into difficulties not to accept any help or assistance whatsoever from anyone other than the Soviet occupying powers but to request the presence of a Soviet Officer which is exactly what he did. At that time the only European nations that recognised the being of the DDR as a separate country were the Soviet Union and the other Warsaw pact members. Any acceptance of assistance from officials of the so-called DDR would signify acceptance of that part of Germany as a separate nation. A Soviet military team did eventually arrive and the sergeant was put back on the road to continue his journey without further incident.

4 BLIGHTY

On return to the UK I found myself posted as an instructor to the 'School' at Wythall. As readers will recall this was the training school previously located at Cheadle in Staffordshire. It was here that airmen who were already qualified Wireless Operators or Telegraphists were undergoing specialist intercept operator training as previously described. Wythall was an old station opening in 1939 as No.6 Barrage Balloon Centre and continued in this role throughout the Second World War. In my time there apart from a small RAF Police unit, No.7 Police District HQ, the school was the only other incumbent unit. The large hangers that in WWII were used to house the inflated balloons when necessary still remained and were rented out to the BMC (British Motor Corporation). These hangers were used by BMC to store new cars that were either yet to be launched on the UK market or exported. The first car I was to see there was the Austin Metropolitan, known also as the Nash Metropolitan, an American designed car built at Longridge in the UK exclusively for export to the USA and Canada although the late Princess Margaret is known to have owned one, no surprise there! We had a good relationship with the BMC workers and quite a few of our number were invited to view these vehicles. The next vehicle to arrive there was the Austin Mini prior to its launch in 1959 and this car did arouse a lot of interest. As readers will know the Mini became somewhat of a revolution in British motoring and remains in production today albeit much updated. A number of my colleagues were fortunate enough to have been allowed a short drive in this car in the vicinity of the hangers, probably the first people ever outside BMC staff to have driven what was to become a British Icon.

Wythall was the second most pleasant and relaxed station on which I was ever to serve. Again like Cheadle before it, bullshit free. It did however sometimes have parades, usually on a Saturday morning which was most inconvenient as they always seemed to be scheduled for the morning after a Friday night function in the Sergeants' Mess.

There was no barrack square or parade ground at Wythall either so this Saturday morning fiasco was held in the school's compound. As a ceremony it was a farce, it was more a case of line up, be inspected then be dismissed to either go back to bed or do whatever one normally did on Saturday mornings. Wythall did have a SWO but one could be forgiven for thinking otherwise, he was rarely seen and certainly very rarely heard. He also had a corporal assistant who must have been very close to the end of his service. A very quiet chap not really suited for a post that involved being responsible for assisting in the administration of discipline and good order. Not long after my arrival this fellow was finally promoted to Sergeant. Soon after this momentous event (for the corporal at least) but not connected with it we held a 'Dining In' night in the Sergeants' mess. This is the occasion when the mess silver comes out to decorate the dining table and all members are dressed in their best bib and tucker with, those that have them, wearing their medals. Another feature is that at the end of the meal, the junior member of the mess is summoned by the CMC (Chairman of the Mess Committee) calling for "Mr Vice" to propose the Loyal Toast. Nothing to it really, this junior member simply stands, raises his glass of port wine which hopefully he has yet to empty, and says, "Gentlemen, (Ladies would of course be included if there were any) The Queen", whereupon all others present, by way of a reply, raise their glasses whilst at the same time repeating, "The Queen". As it happened on this particular occasion, if the SWO's corporal had not been promoted I would have been the junior member but I was happy to find that this was now no longer the case and the duty of Mr Vice would fall upon the new boy, who was however, anything but a boy. During the day, prior to the evening's function the situation was to change when the SWO quietly approached me and asked if I would pretend to be still the junior member of the mess. He explained that his 'lad', being the oldest member present, by age, possibly the oldest person on the station in fact, would have been extremely embarrassed to be singled out in such a way. As I was asked so nicely and in the most pleasant atmosphere that prevailed at Wythall, how could I refuse. That was the first and last time I had to perform that particular duty as on later postings I was never the junior member of the mess.

Although I refer to the mess as the Sergeants' mess its correct title is Warrant Officers' and Sergeants' Mess. I mention this because even on such a small station as Wythall the mess did have a number of Warrant Officer members. One in particular seemed to be the odd one out and he was a grumpy old boy, I suppose every mess must have one. This particular one was the WO in charge of stores. At this time, still a young fellow I had taken to smoking a pipe, no doubt I thought it gave me a sort of distinguished look that would prove attractive to the opposite sex. A young corporal, a fellow instructor also smoked a pipe and he recommended to me that I try a brand of herbal smoking mixture that he was in the habit of buying when home at weekends. Incredibly cheap I seem to remember so I took him up on his offer to purchase some for myself. Following the next weekend he spent at home he dutifully presented me with what seemed like half a hundred weight of this mixture that had the appearance of dried grass but probably weighed no more than a pound and a half . That evening, after dinner in the mess, retiring to the ante room I filled and set light to the pipe settling down to relax and read the daily papers. It was a lovely summer's evening and the windows were open. Very soon loud sniffing sounds interspersed with grunts were heard to come from the direction of 'grumpy' seated in his usual armchair. Eventually, after much more somewhat louder sniffing and grunting grumpy left his chair saying, "That bloody gardener has been burning the grass again" whereupon he went round shutting most of the windows. I almost chewed the stem off my pipe trying to hold in the laughter and others, who knew where the pungent smell, something like a mixture of old dead leaves and horse manure was coming from, either had a large grin on their faces or were chuckling into their newspapers. After that, not wanting to push my luck, I never did light the pipe containing that mixture in the mess again. After all, the day would come when the windows would not be open and the unfortunate gardener could not be held to blame.

At Wythall I was once again in the company of some old friends including the aforementioned Mick Brophy. Mick and I, often in the company of others were to enjoy many an evening out visiting the local hostelries of which there were many, some very pleasantly situated in the beautiful Warwickshire countryside. One such hostelry sticks in mind. This was located in the pretty village of Henley on Arden and lived up to its reputation of serving the best chicken and mushroom pies in the county. This was normally a treat to be enjoyed for Sunday lunch.

At such a relaxed and easygoing station it came as a bit of a blow to hear that the school was soon to move to RAF Digby in Lincolnshire. Digby housed one of Britain's main Y service intercept stations, No.399 SU and was therefore run on stricter and more disciplined lines than we had enjoyed at Wythall. Also located at Digby were a mobile signals unit and the Aerial Erectors' School resulting in it having a fairly large population that included Officers' and other ranks families' accommodation located on site.

This was the period when National Service was still operating and therefore a good number of the students on this 'Y' course were National Service airmen conscripted for a period of two years. They had already spent about six months on their initial basic (square bashing) and Wireless Operator training. Permitted periods of leave and the sixteen weeks they were to spend on this specialist course didn't leave them much time to continue being of use to the Royal Air Force. I suppose however, the theory was that they would be available as reservists should their service be required at some later date. A carrot was dangled in front of these airmen, if they would sign on for an extra year then they would receive the same pay as the regular serving career airmen. Some did take up this offer but there were others who considered that there were better opportunities to be had by continuing in their civilian career. Most of these latter types had had their 'call up' deferred until they were twenty-one and had by then completed the training in their chosen profession. I remember having two such chaps in one class I took. One a qualified dentist and the other a chemist who had a promising career waiting for him with Boots the

Chemist. I am sure that both these chaps, certainly the dentist, could if they so desired, have obtained commissions in the RAF.

Fortunately the move to Digby was not all gloom and doom as I was to meet up with my good friend Tony from my time in Berlin who was now working at 399 SU. We did not take long to rekindle our friendship and continue with our pastime of doing a little bit of hunting or, as I think the local gamekeepers would have put it, poaching. Not quite up to the fabled 'Lincolnshire Poacher' standard but it did provide much meat for our respective tables in the form of rabbits, hares and pheasants. Apart from owning a firearm we had a ferret that we kept, unknown to anyone but ourselves, in an old disused Nissan hut. In addition to supplying meat for our own consumption we were able to supplement our spending money by selling some of the ill-gotten gains to eager trainees to take home at the weekend.

The only non-RAF staff within the school were Mr Brown, a civilian liaison officer from GCHQ. and his secretary a Mrs Chambers. Mr Brown, a likeable fellow, did seem to have a lot of sway as to who went where when further overseas postings became available; indeed it was he who selected me and two others to go to Berlin. Mrs Chambers, I believe a widow, had an interest in vintage cars and owned a rather fine one herself I think it may have been a Daimler. When I bought myself an ex AA Land Rover the said Lady asked if she could have a drive in it in return for me driving her large vintage car. She was a charming person and very well liked by all the staff in the school.

One day Mr Brown summoned me to his office and asked if I would like to go to Australia, would I? Dammed right I would. I knew that we had a small number of RAF Personnel there, seconded to the Australian counterpart of GCHQ, The Defence Signals Branch (DSB) of the Australian Defence Department, later to be renamed Defence Signals Directorate (DSD) and located in Melbourne. I always thought it was only the privileged few who landed that job, now it seemed I was to be one of them.

5 DOWN UNDER

One cold November day in 1960 I journeyed to RAF Innsworth that had now become the PDU, to be issued with any extra items of kit that I may be expected to need in warmer climes. Together with a party of other SNCOs (Senior Non-Commissioned Officers) who were also overseas bound I reported to stores for the issue of these items to take place. It took the usual form beginning with two white kit bags with circular blue lines on them, but not for me. My name was called and instead of the kit bags I was issued with two very nice blue holdalls, one large and one small. This came to me as a surprise and caused some dissension among the others present. They wanted to know why they could not also have these nice posh holdalls but no answer was forthcoming. All I could tell them was that I was off to Australia and presumed such issues were made so that I would not look like the poor relation in the eyes of our Commonwealth opposite numbers. All kitted out and within two days I was off to Stanstead with my family to board a charter flight to Singapore where we were to stay for a few days before boarding a civil aircraft for the next leg of the journey.

After a quick change of airlines in Sydney I was pleased to arrive in Melbourne in the middle of the Australian summer and following a few days settling in to rented accommodation I reported in civilian clothes to DSB located in a barracks complex in Albert Park (now a Formula 1 Race Track). Following a one week handover from the previous incumbent in the post, another RAF Sergeant, I took my place at a desk in company with four other analysts, which is what I had apparently become for this tour. The others including, the senior one who collated our work and who was a New Zealand civilian, a young lady, heavily pregnant and from GCHQ, her husband, also from GCHQ worked in the adjoining office, two Australian civilians made up the numbers. Settling in nicely to the job when the young lady seated opposite seemingly searching for something in her desk drawer that she was not able to find asked me the question, "Have you any Durex?" Needless to say I was somewhat taken aback by this, here was a young, already pregnant lady asking if I had any condoms, a birth control aid known in the UK by that name. A colleague, sensing my embarrassment, and grinning said, "She means Sellotape." Obviously Durex was an Australian brand name for the adhesive tape known to folk in the UK as Sellotape although sold under a number of other brand names. Strange how these become part of ones everyday language, a bit like the word Hoover that is so frequently used when referring to a vacuum cleaner or the act of using one regardless of what brand the machine really is.

For the first time in my career my pay for doing the same job was now approaching that of the civilians alongside me. The reason for this was not that the cut-price spy was no longer such a bargain but because service personnel abroad were always paid an overseas allowance, the amount varying depending on the area employed. Australia, for some reason qualified for a fairly decent allowance of this nature. Added to this was a small clothing allowance because I was required to wear civilian clothes whilst working there.

My boss at the start of my tour at DSB was Squadron Leader Bill Merrick, a really nice chap who, I was later to discover, was the brother of one of my junior schoolteachers. The job to which I was assigned, sitting at a desk all day (with an enjoyable lunch break in one of the many pubs for a 'counter' lunch), sifting through and analysing third-party intercepts from a unit based in Taiwan or Formosa as it was known to us then, wasn't exactly stimulating. True, it did have its moments when something unusual turned up but these moments were rare. One highlight for me was when I came across a puzzling flight pattern that was contained in particular intercept and a chap on the next desk offered to help solve it.

This was no ordinary offer of help, the chap in question was a Royal Australian Air Force pilot and the offer was to take me aloft and fly the pattern that I was finding difficult to analyse. An RAF colleague, one of the six and working in another office would join us and plot the flight on the ground. So, one fine morning it was off to RAAF Station

Laverton on the outskirts of Melbourne. In 1989 Laverton merged with another near-by RAAF Base, Point Cook and was re-named RAAF Williams. Although there remains an RAAF presence at Laverton it ceased to exist as an airfield early in the 1990s when approval was given by the Victorian Government for the land and runway to be turned into a residential suburb to be known as Williams Landing. In my time however, the early 1960s, it was still RAAF Laverton where I was to take my first flight in a military fighter aircraft. This was a De Havilland Vampire T11 jet fighter training aircraft. The seating, for two only, is side-by-side, quite a squeeze. The young airman strapping me in very tightly kept on calling me sir, no doubt because I was wearing one of my hosts flying suits with his rank badges in evidence. Apart from the times that the gravitational force gave me some amount of pain in the ears I did enjoy the short flight. Another 'first' for me during my short visit to Laverton was the sight of a Lockheed U-2 ultra-high altitude reconnaissance aircraft, albeit on the ground. To put icing on the cake this fine pilot, Squadron Leader Gordon Ross bought both my colleague and I a pub lunch afterwards, what a decent fellow. Such a difference to most, but not all, RAF officers I have known, no bullshit, just down to earth and get on with the job. It says so much for the Australian classless society, what a way to live and enjoy life, I came across this repeatedly in Australia and in the East, their Armed Forces Officers, at least the ones I met or worked with, had a genuine interest in the welfare of their troops and therefore gained the respect they deserved.

After about 18 months on that particular desk and wanting a change I opted for a move. A move I was to regret later as the work was just as monotonous and the one GCHQ employee on this desk was less than cooperative. Others on the desk were the head of that department, one young RAF Airman, and one American civilian from the NSA. Apart from the GCHQ fellow we all got along very well together and the American, one other RAF Sergeant and I spent many a pleasant lunchtime together. We even managed to introduce the 'yank' to the game of badminton that led to us enjoying some evenings in each others company. This friendship did, on one occasion, have an added advantage when the breweries in Melbourne went on strike. Yes! Unbelievable, Australia without beer, Strewth! This time the USA came to the rescue, our colleague was able to obtain duty free supplies via his embassy and supplied us with our needs, to be paid back when local supplies returned to normal. I seem to remember this took about a week, a week during which much of Melbourne was mourning the loss, albeit temporarily, of their favourite amber liquid.

The social life there more than compensated for lack of activity and excitement not inherent in the job. Lots of sun and time spent on the beach or in the sea snorkel diving and spear fishing, all the fish we took from the sea were either eaten or given to others to eat. We would also sometimes gather mussels and give them to small parties of, mostly elderly, so-called New Australians, in this case Italians or Greeks that had come down to the beach. These folk would be looking for mussels closer to the shore but those that were available to them were close to a dirty water outlet pipe and not the healthiest of fare so they were more than pleased to accept any that we gathered a little further out from the shore. We had our share of scares when taking part in this activity in the coastal waters south-east of Melbourne. At he height of summer, in addition to the life guards present on raised platforms on the beach a small aircraft would fly around spotting for sharks. At any sight of these creatures, which, in Australia always seemed very aggressive, a siren would sound and everyone would rapidly exit the water. Early one morning when a friend and I were enjoying a spot of rod and line fishing from some cliffs above a small yacht basin we noticed a fellow and a small child enter the water. Almost at the same time we became aware that some of the boats and sailing dinghies anchored there in the calm water were being disturbed and were rocking from side to side. The cause of this disturbance soon became apparent, the water there was shallow and a large shark was making its way toward the beach, bumping into some of the boats en-route. After some frantic shouting and arm waving from the two of us, although he did hesitate and appeared to wonder what the hell we were shouting for, he quickly gathered up the child and returned to the safety of the beach.

In my teenage days living in North Wales I had always been keen on doing a bit of shooting, mostly rabbits for the table. Here in Australia where, in those days one did not require a licence or any form of permit to own small calibre firearms providing they were not concealable weapons, pistols or revolvers I was able to purchase a very fine Walther .22 calibre rifle and seek out opportunities to use it. It is now to my shame that when such an opportunity did come my way in the form of a trip up into New South Wales I was glad to take it. I say to my shame because these days I am loath to kill anything, even insects. I do make an exception with wasps though if they are likely to be threatening as their sting has a serious effect on my well-being. I disposed of any firearms I had many years ago. A good number of people I have known have shared this experience of having a complete change of heart as they became older. I think also that the effect over the years of meeting so many other different thinking people and in some cases the effect of certain events in ones life can also bring about this change. However, in the Australian summer of 1962 I was yet to be affected in this way and took advantage of an offer to go north and do some shooting.

My companions on this, my first and only journey into the Australian bush, were an RAF colleague at DSB, Jim Hall and an Australian lad, Rod' with whom I had become friendly and who had been on a previous hunting trip to the area. Rod' kindly took us, although we shared the driving, to a large, 35,000-hectare sheep station close to the small village of Maude some miles across the Victorian State border and into New South Wales. Here we were introduced to the manager/owner of the sheep station who gave us permission to camp and shoot on their property. Following our long, hot and tiring journey from Melbourne we were happy to set up camp alongside the Murrumbidgee River, the second largest in Australia and a tributary of the longer Murray River. For two weeks this river was to be our only source of drinking water and our place to wash, both our clothes and ourselves. A shady spot was chosen under a number of very large Gum (eucalyptus) trees. Tents were not required at that time of the year hammocks slung between two trees or a sleeping bag was all that one needed. Much of this large property consisted of bush and scrub that was inhabited by wild pig, foxes, kangaroos and a large number of smaller mammals. Obviously being a sheep station with many thousand sheep there also had to be a large amount of pasture land. The remainder was mainly very dry and akin to desert where emus, rabbits, in great numbers and kangaroos, when outside the cover of the bush, could be seen. It was in this arid area that we were to do our night time shooting by the light of a large spotlight attached to the top of the vehicle's cab. Venturing out in the dark but usually starry night it never ceased to amaze me how we found our way back to our pitch. It was difficult enough in daytime without a compass or any other navigational aid. I certainly would never have been able to but Rod' never seemed to have any problem, his navigation was spot on and we never got lost once. When asked about this he said he used the stars but I rather think it was his sixth sense, he always seemed to know exactly where he was and where he was going.

Camping beside the river was fine until we decided that it was mealtime, not a fly in sight until then. As soon as food was on ones plate hordes of the little black beasts would descend, I have no idea just where they all came from. Almost at once, it became difficult to take a spoon or fork-full of food without gathering half a dozen flies along with it. We coped with this in different ways. For me it was relatively simple, my hammock was the type that had a built in mosquito net so all I had to do was unzip the side entrance stick my upper body in there together with plate of food and continue with my meal, albeit in the standing position. My two colleagues, without the luxury of hammocks, didn't have it quite so easy but did manage by cocooning themselves with a large towel over the head together with the meal on the plate. The simple answer to all this soon became obvious and that was only to have the main meal of the day after dark sitting around the fire that we had used to cook the meal. We may have been hungry during the day but it was worth it to have a meal in relative peace later.

We had been settled in this spot beside the river a very short while when a couple of young Australian lads from New South Wales decided to also camp a short distance away. They had only been there an hour or so when one approached asking if we had shot a large black snake at which he was then pointing. No, we had not shot a snake and further investigation revealed that said snake had not been shot but was just lying there soaking up the sun, quite close to both our pitches. These two fellows were quite knowledgeable regarding such reptiles and informed us that this particular one was indeed deadly. We were to see many snakes during our short stay there, most of them, according to our new neighbours, were venomous with a bite that could prove fatal. Early one evening we were to see a large number of black snakes heading in our direction by swimming across the river. Bearing in mind what we had been told we were not taking any chances and .22 rifles were brought into use against what had the appearance of an invading army. When shot and we were able to see their under-parts, these snakes, although jet-black on sight were a bright yellow colour underneath. This led Jim to remark that they looked like so much spaghetti, not a meal I would have fancied. I don't imagine for one moment that these creatures were indeed intent on attacking, it was just unfortunate that along that stretch of the river there were so many places they could have chosen to come ashore. Why they chose the relatively short space that we were occupying remains a mystery, but sadly for them we did not fancy sharing our spot with them when we were walking around in shorts and most of the time bare-footed or with only minimum protection on the feet. Added to this of course, my two companions, slept in sleeping bags on the ground, brave lads.

With so many empty .22 brass cartridge cases on hand considering the amount of ammunition we had expended it seemed a pity not to make some use of them. To this end we hammered a quantity of them into the trunk of a very large tree on the riverbank in the shape of both Jim's and my name with the title RAF beneath. No doubt by now with the growth of the tree the brass will have fallen out but would have left indentations in place marking our presence in this beautiful part of New South Wales.

Sometimes in the early evening we would see a small number of wild duck flying downstream. Thinking that duck would make a nice change from rabbit or whatever else we had been feeding on it was decided to take a pot shot the next time any came our way. Standing on the riverbank, stripped off and about to take a quick dip I was alerted to the sight of a pair of ducks heading in our direction. Grabbing the shotgun that was a 5-shot 12 bore FN automatic, I fired two shots before the ducks were out of sight and did manage to hit one of them. The problem then was how the hell do we retrieve it from the very fast flowing river. There was nothing else that could be done except to rapidly plunge into the river and go for it. This I did and managed to grab the unfortunate very dead duck from mid-stream, now to return to the riverbank. Easier said than done. As I said, this river was very fast flowing, I am not, and never was, the strongest of swimmers. It soon became obvious that I needed two hands and both arms to make it to the bank and the duck occupied one hand. Nothing for it but to do what a good four-legged retriever would do, take duck in mouth. I must have been crazy, once my mouth was stuffed with feathers, which were also going up my nose breathing became difficult. So, by then being not too far away from the riverbank, if somewhat much farther downstream, I removed duck from mouth and hurled it toward the shore. My luck held and our potential meal landed safely. Was it worth the effort? No, has to be the answer one small duck between three did not make a meal. This exercise was not repeated, one unfortunate creature had lost its life and because of my stupidity I could have been close to losing mine in the river. For much of the rest of our diet we relied upon the ground dwelling animals we shot, rabbit, wild pig and a fillet of kangaroo that was also taken for its pelt.

For other necessary supplies and much needed refreshment we would journey into Maude. The village itself consisted of just a few buildings alongside the narrow road that passed through there. At that time the buildings were a combined grocery store and filling station, a school and a pub. Many happy times were spent in the pub that was owned by an Englishman from, if my memory serves me right, Blackburn or some other Lancashire town close to there. He was a nice chap who informed us that he would be happy to cash cheques for me should we have any difficulties with such formalities at the grocery store. As it happened, although the store owner didn't see many cheques he was also quite happy to accept same. One afternoon, after a fair amount of liquid refreshment I went to move from the bar and almost fell flat on my face. One of my two companions, unknown to me, had fastened a genuine but very old, very heavy and a trifle rusty, ball and chain around my ankle. This instrument was obviously something left over from the days of the convict gangs in Australia and was kept as an item of interest or amusement for tourists or others passing through the village. On another occasion, again after downing a fair quantity of delicious ice-cold beer Jim decided that he needed a haircut. Borrowing a pair of scissors from behind the bar I was happy to oblige. Of course I had no idea how to go about such a delicate operation so I simply attacked his thatch taking chunks out of it here and there. The effect was rather patchwork but I'm happy to say that by the time we returned to Melbourne it was not too noticeable. The nearest town of any size was Hay, some 30 miles, (about 50kms) from Maud to where we journeyed one day just to drink a pint of fresh milk, something that for some reason did not seem to be available in Maude. Hay itself has a very interesting history of which I don't believe any of us were aware of at the time we were there.

During WWII Hay was the location of internment and prisoner of war camps. Three high-security camps were constructed there in 1940. The first occupants of one of these camps were over two thousand refugees from Nazi Germany and Austria. They arrived in Australia on the HMT Dunera, a troopship that I well remember being on the Far East routes when I was stationed in Hong Kong. They arrived in Hay in September 1940 and remained there until May 1941 when they were transferred elsewhere. Many of these refugees were to settle in Australia at the war's end. Also accommodated in these camps at one time were Japanese POWs and Italian internees, both POWs and civilians.[24]

At the end of an unforgettable two weeks we set out on our return journey to Melbourne from NSW. It was, as I recall hot and dusty and we did have a few 'refreshment' stops en-route. During one of these stops, as I was at this time still smoking a pipe and no doubt still thinking it made me appear distinguished, I called into a grocery store to replenish my tobacco, the days of the herbal smoking mixture were well behind me. Not sure where this was but I think it was Deniliquin close to the border with the state of Victoria. There I purchased what appeared to be pipe tobacco; at least the packet bore a name I was familiar with at the time. I didn't have a lot of choice really as this solitary pack seemed to be the only one on the shelf that I could see. Opening this pack the next time I decided to light up I found that all I had was what looked and felt like a few dried up twigs among a handful of dust. The store I bought it from, well, it did look like something from the dim and distant past, but the tobacco must have been reclining there on that shelf since the days of the gold rush in the mid nineteenth century. I had to wait a little longer for a puff of the pipe.

All the single or unaccompanied married RAF personnel at DSB were accommodated in lodgings on Beach Road, Blackrock. As the name of the road suggests this was on the coast road and about 11 miles (18km) south-east of Melbourne, a pleasant location directly opposite the beach. The landlady of this establishment looked after the boarders very well and also did their laundry. One day, shortly after our return from the hunting trip, Jim donned one of his newly laundered shirts and discovered to his surprise and horror a very neat bullet hole through one of the sleeves. Luck was with him on two counts on this occasion. One, that the sleeves of the shirt were very baggy and two, apart from the shot gun, we were using nothing larger than .22 calibre rifle ammunition, otherwise, anything larger and the missile would certainly have at least, grazed his arm. As it was we did wonder how he had never felt anything at all. Discussing this among ourselves later we came to the conclusion that it can only have happened at the time we were chasing after some wild pig whilst standing in the back of the pick-up truck, a 'Ute' in Aussie language, travelling at speed over some very uneven ground when our shooting was probably somewhat erratic. I would of course prefer to think that it was more likely to have occurred when Jim was not wearing the shirt. After doing our laundry in the river we would hang the washing on trees to dry so it could well have happened at such a time, if not so then Jim certainly had a lucky escape.

Jim was later to marry a young lady that worked in the same building as ourselves at DSB. Margery was a Radio Operator, a member of the WRANS (Women's Royal Australian Naval Service) and came from Boulder in Western Australia, a lovely girl. They were married in a small chapel just around the corner from where I rented a house in the Blackrock suburb of Melbourne and where they held their small reception. I was a witness at the wedding and the first thing that struck me when I was signing the certificate was the professions of their respective fathers as stated on the form. Jim was from Northumberland in N E England and his father was listed as a Coal Miner, Margery's father; a Gold Miner!

Following the incident of the bullet hole in the shirtsleeve, but not because of it, our shooting was restricted to target practice on Saturday afternoons as members of the Victorian Sporting Shooters Association. This association had a fairly large membership and they were certainly a very friendly bunch. One member had a collection of about five or six semi-automatic weapons including an FN 7.62mm rifle, or to give it its equivalent civil designation .308 Winchester. This rifle was at that time not yet on issue to the British Armed Forces as far as I can remember, certainly not the RAF anyway although it did eventually become standard issue and remained so for many years. I was delighted therefore when invited to put a couple of rounds down the range from this particular weapon. The owner of these weapons would often invite other members to try one or more of his collection, a thoroughly nice fellow. Both my friend Jim and myself were to receive medals for our prowess on the range with this association, I'm afraid with all the moves I have made since those days I no longer have mine but I believe Jim still has his.

There was yet another trip into NSW but this time an official one organised by the service chiefs at DSB and the journey was by air. Civil Air as it happens, the leg from Melbourne to Sydney in a Lockheed Electra and then on to Newcastle in a DC3, Dakota. My first and only flight ever in what had been the workhorse of the air following WWII when many fledgling civil airlines were to equip with Dakotas, mostly former USAF, machines. The particular aircraft in a civil airline livery that we travelled in may well have been a former military version but I don't think I gave that any thought at the time. I was the only RAF member of the party on this journey, the others were one RAAF Flight Sergeant, one UK civilian and a couple of RAAF officers. The purpose of the visit that was to last for a week was to observe various aspects of an exercise that was to take place at, and in the air, around RAAF Station Williamtown, 15kms from Newcastle, which incidentally shared its runway with the Civil airport at which we had arrived. The scenario was that a number of Canberra bombers, I think from RAAF Amberley about 50kms SW of Brisbane in Queensland, were to make simulated bombing attacks on targets in NSW. A squadron of Dassault Mirage fighter aircraft, at Williamtown were the aircraft tasked with the job of intercepting these bombers. The exercise had a realistic feel to it and we were for some of the time to stand close to the runway and observe the fighters being 'scrambled' and rapidly getting airborne in pursuit of the invaders. Time was also spent in the control room where we were to listen to the conversations between the control tower and the fighter pilots as they were vectored on to the targets. Prior to the commencement of the exercise we were seated in a classroom to await a briefing by one of the pilots taking part. This fellow, a tall blonde Flight Lieutenant entered the room dressed in his flying suit and standing before us introduced himself by saying, in a strong German accent, "my name is Hans" I think we were all a little more than surprised by this. Of course we should not have been, this was 1963 and Australia had been accepting immigrants from all over Europe for a good number of years. It just seemed somewhat bizarre at the time, here we were about to witness a situation, albeit simulated, where aircraft were coming to drop bombs close by and a number of fighters were about to shoot these bombers out of the sky. And here was Hans, a German, giving the briefing.

When my tour 'Down Under' came to an end I was hoping to journey home on a nice passenger liner, calling at exotic ports en-route as some before me had done. The only sacrifice required was to forfeit a portion of ones disembarkation leave to make up the time that one would not be available to the RAF by being at sea for a number of weeks. I don't know what had happened in the past but I suspect that either someone had been rather naughty on one of these voyages or it was simply a cost-cutting exercise. Whatever the reason, this travel option was unfortunately no longer available when it came my turn to return to the UK. At least it was civil air all the way.

6 KONFRONTASI

Back in the UK once more and not expecting another overseas posting for at least two years the next 'offer' came as quite a surprise. I barely had time to settle in to another spell as an instructor at RAF Digby when the call came for experienced operators to take an aptitude test to determine if they were suitable candidates to learn a foreign language.

In 1963 President Sukarno of Indonesia decided he didn't want the so-called Puppet State of Malaysia (his words) on his doorstep. Malaysia had been created by the amalgamation of the Federation of Malaya and Singapore (West Malaysia), The British protectorates of North Borneo (later renamed Sabah) and Sarawak (known together and usually referred to as British Borneo and now East Malaysia). Singapore was expelled from the newly formed state of Malaysia in August 1965 and Brunei never did join the Malaysian Federation. By armed aggression Sukarno then took steps to oppose its formation. He believed the newly formed state to be a continuation of British colonial presence in the area and following an unsuccessful incursion into Brunei, small parties of regular and irregular troops were sent into Borneo (Sarawak and Sabah, known in Indonesia as *Kalimantan*) to carry out terrorist raids and spread propaganda. This was the beginning of the armed conflict, *Konfrontasi* or Confrontation as it became known and was to last a further three years.

This initial action was followed in 1964 by raids on the Malaya Peninsular (now known as West Malaysia). Presumably it was at this time that Malaysia asked for assistance from the British and Australian governments in fighting off the aggressor.

Following this request from Malaysia someone, possibly at MOD (Ministry of Defence) realising that Indonesia had a lot of Soviet hardware in the form of aircraft and missiles thought that here was an opportunity not to be missed. As Soviet security was tight and extremely efficient it was not always easy to obtain intelligence on their weapons or equipment. With such hardware in the hands of, and in use by, a less tight-lipped target there was now a heaven sent chance of the task being made much easier. All that was needed was a mobile sigint unit staffed by competent operators with foreign language skills. Sigint facilities had long been in operation in Singapore in the form of a station administered jointly by GCHQ and DSB Melbourne and known as Chai Keng 2 or CK2. This facility was manned by British and Commonwealth civilian personnel together with a number of Commonwealth service personnel. CK2 was however, only capable of intercepting the radio communications of long-range targets within the HF (High Frequency) bands. If short-range transmissions were to be 'captured' then there was now clearly a need for a mobile facility capable of operating within the VHF/UHF or 'line of sight' range of specified targets.

To fill this gap in the system it was decided to form an RAF mobile signals unit to operate in an air-portable go anywhere role. No problems here except that the RAF did not, at that time have any personnel able to fulfil the requirements of such a unit. There were of course a large number of experienced Special Operators (Telegraphy) on hand who were more than capable of meeting the long-range requirement but no Indonesian language trained personnel to undertake the short-range voice commitment. The obvious solution was to quickly train up some of the existing Spec Ops and ship them out east ASAP.

Following language aptitude tests at RAF Digby, six personnel comprising three senior NCOs and three Airmen were selected for language training. The UK venue for a four-week 'lead in' course was to be Chelsea Barracks in London. On completion this was to be followed by a further five months intensive training in Singapore. The reason for selecting this prime London location was twofold. One, Chelsea Barracks had a suitable classroom and, two, a London based native Indonesian tutor was found to be available.

We, the chosen six, were instructed to find our own accommodation in London, take with us only civilian clothes and report to Chelsea Barracks on a certain date in January 1964. On arrival there it seems that we were expected and were directed without ceremony to the education section where we were left to our own devices. We were not to be alone for long though as we were soon joined by a number of British Army NCOs and one officer. The officer, a captain seemed to be the only one who knew what our programme was to be and had been designated i/c (in charge of) discipline and good order by MOD. In addition there were two RAF Officers, DSB Melbourne bound and one Lieutenant Commander RN.

It soon transpired that we would not be meeting our tutor until 1500 hours each day but the gallant Captain decreed that we should all arrive on site by 0900 hours daily and undertake private study. A little difficult this as, until our tutor appeared on the scene, we would have nothing to study. When said chap did arrive we were pleased that he turned out to be a really charming happy smiling fellow whom I will refer to as Alfred although this was not his real name. He never once queried our reasons for wanting to learn the Indonesian Language and for this we were thankful. Should he have been of a curious nature it could have made for a very difficult, or at least, a somewhat embarrassing situation. He quickly recommended that the only learning aid we would need for this, our 'lead in' course was an Indonesian-English Dictionary by Echols & Shadily, published in the USA by Cornell University Press. One of our number was quickly despatched across London to Foyles' bookshop to obtain copies for us at our own expense. I think we were all surprised that any bookshop, even one with such a reputation as this, would have sufficient copies but fortunately for everyone concerned, they did.

Each day Alfred would attempt to instil into our brains a considerable amount of vocabulary in a variety of simple ways. Grammar didn't matter he said, get the words in first, plenty time for grammar later, how right that turned out to be. At the end of each day Alfred would give us thirty words to be learnt by the next day. What happened if one didn't learn all thirty in the allotted time one may ask? Simple, one was given another 30 the next day to add to the total.

Alfred's philosophy was straightforward; "you all want to go to Singapore don't you?" "Then, you help me and I will help you". As it was up to Alfred to make the final decision as to whether each individual was proficient enough to go on to further training at the end of four weeks, everyone made a determined effort at this stage. One exercise in the short course involved the students inventing a phrase or sentence and translating it into Indonesian. All went well until someone used the sentence, "the boy threw a stick for the dog". No problem here one would think, Alfred did have a problem with this though, saying, "You have said, the boy threw a stick for the dog, it should be, the boy threw a stick at the dog". "That is not what I meant," replied the student, "I said for the dog and that is what I meant to say". "But why would one want to throw a stick for a dog", said Alfred. "In order that it could return it to me," said the student. Now Alfred really was confused, especially after being told that the stick would be returned so that it could continue to be thrown for the dog to retrieve yet again. The exchange went on in this vein for a little while longer until the exasperated student simply gave up. As we all know, those in the Western World play games with dogs whereas such frivolity is rare in the developing world where sticks and other missiles are more likely to be hurled in the direction of the unfortunate beast.

The mornings allotted to private study were often interspersed by much gazing out of the window observing the activities in and around the parade ground below. Young subalterns (known as Ensigns in the Guards I believe) wandering around in brown boots with highly polished black toe caps and beating hell out of their left leg with a swagger stick. This when they were allowed to walk around alone, most of the time they seemed to be marched around accompanied by a smart but burly Guards NCO. Another diversion was the presence of Sir Richard Attenbourgh, parking his nice shiny Rolls Royce (registration RA1) alongside the hallowed parade ground on a number of days whilst he observed the rehearsals for the Colour Trooping ceremony. He was, apparently, boning up for the role of Sergeant Major he was soon to play in the film, Guns at Batasi, not, according to some critics, one of his best.

Many lunch times were something of a gastronomic delight, at least the ORs (Other Ranks) among us thought so as we were to frequent a wonderful, cramped and steamy Greek basement restaurant just around the corner from the barracks. Excellent food washed down with a glass of Retsina and for some, a snort of Ouzo. I must add that this did not happen every day, which is just as well, having to remain compos mentis to await Alfred's arrival later in the day. The proprietor, a jolly corpulent Greek fellow was more than generous, sometimes supplying extra titbits at no extra cost and saying, "if you haven't got the money, pay me next time". OK, so this last remark may have been a typical Mediterranean ploy to make sure we came back again but the offer was there and he was not to know how itinerant we were and therefore whether or not there would indeed be a 'next time'.

Part way through the course another tutor arrived on the scene in the form of a Malay national. As there are only minor differences between the Indonesian and Malay languages no doubt someone making the decisions thought that this chap would fill in some of the time that Alfred could not. This newcomer was I believe, employed in a diplomatic role on behalf of his country and was related to a well-known personage in the Malaysian government of the day. Unlike Alfred, he was of an inquisitive nature and queried our reasons for wanting to learn Indonesian. One would have thought that this was obvious given the prevailing situation in South East Asia, with him being Malay and therefore 'on our side' as it were. It seems he wasn't very well informed or perhaps his superiors were following a strict need-to-know policy and not letting all and sundry (even their diplomats) know that they couldn't get along without help from their former colonial masters! I don't think he was entirely convinced with our explanations to the effect that we were off to South East Asia and wanted to learn something of at least one of the languages of the region purely out of interest but he did not pursue the matter further, much to our relief.

The course was successfully completed by all the students and celebrated together with Alfred, in a pub adjacent to Sloan Square underground station before heading for our lodgings (which for some was the Union Jack Club opposite Waterloo Station) to pack our bags and head off home. Following a brief spell at home it was off to RAF Lynham in Wiltshire to board a service aircraft bound for Singapore.

As most ex-servicemen will remember, the first port-of-call when arriving on any unit or station is the Orderly Room and this was where the secret six found themselves when they arrived at Royal Air Force Station Seletar in Singapore in March 1964. The brief for these six airmen, One Chief Technician, two Sergeants one Corporal and two Senior Aircraftmen was to further their knowledge of the Indonesian language and assist in the formation of a mobile signals unit. After being handed the ubiquitous arrival form [25] or blue chit, as it was known they enquired as to the location of No. 54 Signals Unit. "Oh, it's in the old band hut, down by the swimming pool, we think" was the reply from an orderly room clerk.

Setting off down the road in the tropical heat and humidity and wearing their newly pressed and starched khaki drill uniforms, now rapidly being reduced by sweat to something akin to wet dish cloths, they sought out the band hut. None of them having any idea what to expect when said hut was located. Consequently, what they did find came as no small surprise. Espying a small brick built building adjacent to a larger one housing the station's wireless transmitters they could hear the sound of someone playing a tune on a wind instrument. "Ah" remarked one of the party, "that must be the place", he must have been the brightest member of the group. Further investigations revealed a somewhat dejected Warrant Officer nursing a cornet, no, not of the ice cream variety but the previously heard musical instrument. With the arrival of these six moonies (anyone newly arrived in the East was known as a moonie because of his pale complexion) the WO stopped playing and queried the reason for this visitation. Upon being informed that this party were seeking 54 Signals Unit the musician replied, "You've found it, this is it, and you have kicked me out of my band hut".

With that, putting away his cornet he slowly departed the scene never to be seen in that vicinity again.

The question now was what to do with a sparsely furnished hut and a place where there was no other sign of life except for the screaming, sounds of splashing and jollification coming from the swimming pool about 150 metres distant along the road. Investigations in that area would have to wait so the six merry men did what all other good airmen would do, they set of to find something to eat and drink and somewhere to bed down, then skive away the rest of the day best they could. To achieve the first two aims would of course necessitate the completion of the arrival chit so it was off to find places where signatures were to be obtained. All this completed it was off to feed, slurp a glass or two of the famous Tiger beer then crash out for the remainder of the afternoon, after all, this was the tropics. The second visit to what had been, until now, the musical hub of the station would have to wait until the next day, and maybe more would then be revealed

Sure enough, on a visit to the former band hut the next day we were to discover that an OC (Officer Commanding) had been appointed and had arrived on station. This officer, a Flight Lieutenant, whom I shall refer to as Flt.Lt X was an ex-ranker who had actually served at Seletar many years previous in the rank of Flight Sergeant. He was of the engineering variety and although he was most likely aware of the type of operations the unit was to carry out he was not, to begin with, Au fait with the skills and methods used by trained sigint operators in such situations as we shall see when we come to the incident at Marina Hill. This was of course, typical of the way the system operated at that time. Any officer would do to take charge of a unit providing he could sign his name to official documents, even if he only had a vague idea what was in them. Thankfully, I am led to believe this has now all changed and officers experienced in sigint are being appointed to command such units.

Flt.Lt X however, did have some knowledge of antennae and was quite enthusiastic about such things. Just as well really as we were later to need a good number of antennae varying in shape and size. All very well, but what about the remainder of the operation? It is indeed good to have a technical brain at the helm but the day-to-day operations needed some thoughtful consideration. The three Senior NCOs were well capable of running the show, relying on the co-operation and skills of others but, following the line that only officers could be at the top of the tree, an operations officer was appointed. Hurrah! This time they got it right, well almost. The gentleman appointed to this post was a Chinese Linguist, one of the first trained as such in those days and experienced in sigint. Flying Officer Peter Cousins was known to at least two of the party from his days as a Junior Technician at RAF Little Sai Wan, Hong Kong in the 1950s.

Now that personnel seemed to be arriving to staff the unit, all that was needed was equipment. First of all though, the six detailed to further their language studies for the next five months would need transport. A short-wheelbase Land Rover was quickly obtained from the station's MT section and trips to the British Army's Nee Soon Barracks some 8 miles (13km) or so distant was commenced on a daily basis.

Arriving at Nee Soon Barracks and being told where to sit in the classroom it soon became obvious that this course was to be run on strict military lines. We were seated in 'horseshoe' shape with the officers and senior ranks on the ends of the horseshoe therefore closest to the instructor. With the opening of the first lesson following introductions there was a distinct feeling that the instructor, a Major Parrot, would be biased toward the Army students.

The Major was not the most patient of tutors and whilst he may have been a fine officer and soldier, in my opinion his teaching skills left much to be desired. He was however, assisted by a Malaysian Army Staff Sergeant, Abdul Rahman, a likeable chap. Without this native senior NCO at his side I think the Major would have struggled as he was often to turn to him for confirmation in the use of words or sentences.

Alongside the road leading into the barracks were a number of permanently sited market stalls the owners of which were hoping to persuade the soldiery to buy their wares. All manner of souvenirs were on display, many of them just tat that would undoubtedly one day finish up in the dustbin in the UK. One stall specialised in aids allegedly designed to increase ones sexual pleasure or performance. The labels on such items that, in addition to the title and description, included detailed instructions in their use. All these details were in Chinese or Malay, sometimes both but Malay was the dominant language. As there are only minor differences between the Malay and Indonesian language we found little difficulty in chatting to the locals and reading the script. At that time there were a number of differences in the spelling of some words but the meanings did not change. In the 1970s an agreement was reached between the two countries to standardise the spellings. In the main the result favoured the Malay spellings.

A couple of months into the course, one of our members, Dennis, when browsing the objects on this particular stall was approached by the owner and asked if he would be interested in doing some translation work on the product labels. As we took every opportunity to practice our language skills this owner was well aware of our abilities so Dennis agreed to the proposal and was told he could choose any item he wanted from the stall in return for his labours. One item was a small bottle containing clear liquid to be applied to the male genitals in order to increase ones performance in the bedroom. Dennis confided in me saying that he had some difficulty translating this description into English that the target customers would understand so he ended up simply calling it 'Knob Hardener'. No doubt the stall owners sales shot up after this. I can't recall Dennis accepting anything for his efforts but I do know that he found most product descriptions amusing and enjoyed doing the translations.

After five months the course came to an end and it was time to take the final aural examination. As expected the candidates to be tested were chosen in rank and service order. Therefore, once the officers of all three services had been tested all the Army personnel took priority over the RAF personnel regardless of rank. I was the last of the RAF contingent to be successfully tested, the Chief Technician and the other sergeant went before me. I passed without too much trouble and Staff Sergeant Rahman seemed pleased with my efforts. One particular sentence I was to use in reply to a question baffled the Major but 'Staff' assured him that what I had said was correct and in very good Indonesian. The RAF junior ranks were to follow but it was here that the Major gave up and called a halt to proceedings saying they were not up to it and needed further tuition. How he could have arrived at this decision after a few brief moments with only one of the junior ranks is beyond me. This officer was later to make known his opinions to one of our senior officers at Headquarters Far East Air Force (HQ FEAF). He stated that he believed that the RAF students did not have the same expertise as did the Army personnel. Of course, whilst he may have been aware of the reason for the Army students learning Indonesian he was certainly not aware of the reasons for the RAF students so doing. He was not indoctrinated into the world of sigint so there was no reason for him to know. The whole situation smacked of 'sour grapes'. He may also have been well impressed by the talents of at least two of the army students. One, a WO2 (Warrant Officer Class 2) was and had been for many years married to a Malay, at home when not on duty he lived like a Malay and spoke only Malay in the house. Little wonder that he was the star of the course. Another, a Sergeant was on his second tour in Malaysia and had a long term Malay girl friend. He was also to find the course something of a walk in the park.

As a celebration following the course it was decided to go for a typical Malay meal in one of the restaurants in Singapore frequented by Malay Nationals. I seem to remember that there were no knives and forks supplied, the authenticity went all the way and we had to eat with hands, I should say with one hand only, the right one; the left one being placed firmly in ones lap. I do know that the meal was enjoyed by most and it was in the early hours of the following day before some of us climbed into our beds.

Some months later when I was being de-briefed at CK2 I was surprised to see Major Parrot being given a conducted tour of the set room and I was greeted with a friendly smile. At last someone had decided to indoctrinate him and put him in the picture. I would hope that from then on he would view any RAF students in a different light.

Meanwhile, back at base, more staff were starting to arrive to man the unit which still did not have the vehicles necessary to bring its operations up to strength. Soon in situ were; 1 Sergeant Wireless Fitter, 1 SAC Wireless Mechanic, 1 Corporal Aerial Erector, 1 SAC Aerial Erector, 1 Sergeant MT Fitter, 1 Sergeant Electrician, 1 SAC Supplier (Storeman), 1 Corporal Nursing Attendant, 2 SAC Wireless Operators and 2 SAC Cooks. At first many thought that there were three cooks, one named Mick Jennings and the other McInernie hence, Mick, Mack and Ernie.

Whilst waiting for our vehicles to arrive from the UK we were supplied with a Morris J2 Van and a 3-Ton Bedford truck to give the unit some sort of mobile operational capability. The language course kept us in school from 0800 hours until 1300 hours daily. Following a lunch break we would report to the unit where we began to see things taking shape. Some building work was taking place to make the former band hut fit for purpose and a separate small building was being added to serve as an operations block. This would comprise an air-conditioned 'set room,' containing desks upon which to install radio receivers, a small office where the analysis of intercepted wireless traffic would take place and where briefings could be held. A storeroom and new toilet facilities were also added to the side of this block. These buildings were by this time surrounded by a chain link fence with large double gates to facilitate the movement of vehicular traffic. A small side gate in sight of, and electronically controlled from, inside the main building was also fitted into the fence. To gain entry via this side gate one had to press a bell-push then entry would only be permitted when one was recognised by someone in the building. On one occasion a European in civilian clothes accompanied by two young Malays rang the bell. This 'comedian', when questioned as to his reasons for wanting entry to the compound replied to the effect that he was from P&SS (Provost and Security Services) at Changi and had come to take our Secret Waste for destruction. Oh yes indeed! What did those RAF Police types take us for? These 'visitors' were quickly sent packing and the Seletar RAF Police were informed of their presence on the station. We were later to receive confirmation that the party were, as they stated from the RAF Police unit at RAF Changi. Our own station Police knew us too well to try such an amateur stunt.

At this stage the Morris J2 was being fitted out with radio receivers, two R216 VHF and two Racal RA17HF. The RA17 became a replacement throughout the sigint world for the HRO and I must say proved itself an excellent choice, certainly the finest set I was to use following the HRO. This fitting out of the Morris J2 was of course only a stopgap measure to enable us to test the water as it were and keep us off the streets. On a few occasions we would take this J2 to Marina Hill, a patch of high ground in the south west of Singapore Island. Although we were able to hear some Indonesian signals traffic from this location little of it was of great interest. It did however, allow us to check our antennae set up knowing that a similar configuration would be used in addition to much larger arrays elsewhere. To do this we would track the flights of civil aircraft in and out of Paya Lebar, at that time Singapore's International airport. This gave us some idea of the range we could expect from this limited VHF facility. In addition to this and giving the aerial erectors a chance to display their skills, the Marina Hill trips gave others a chance to try their hand at making and erecting a makeshift shower from a pair of plastic buckets and installing an Elsan chemical toilet. These essential facilities were suitably screened with Hessian sacking attached to poles.

Reporting to Marina Hill one afternoon following a mornings language training at Nee Soon the six Spec Ops were amazed to be greeted by Flt Lt X, our OC who said something to the effect, "I don't know what we need you 'specialist' types for, look what McDonald has done". With that he showed us, with a flourish, a page of a log on which we would normally use for transcribing our intercepted radio traffic. Jim McDonald, one of our two 'straight' as opposed to specialist, Wireless Operators, had written down details of a Morse transmission he had intercepted. The page of the log had spaces on it for all the details of the intercept, time, date, frequency, operators ID and comments, indeed all the items essential for an analyst to transcribe and make some intelligent sense of the intercept. Jim had not completed any such details or left the spaces blank, he had simply written right across the log from left to right as one would on a piece of scrap paper and, as such, this intercept would have been completely worthless. Not his fault, he had not undergone the sixteen weeks of specialist training that Spec Ops had, in addition of course he had no knowledge of the Indonesian Language that would have given him some idea of what he was intercepting. This is just one example of the folly of appointing officers to command a unit operating in a field in which they had no previous experience or training.

Still waiting for the Land Rovers, (although we had retained the one used for the school runs) and now that the language course had been completed and the successful students had received their bounty [26] the 'Boss' decided a detachment 'Up Country' would be in order. The chosen venue for this first real operational detachment albeit with limited transport and equipment was Changkat. Not to be confused with the other Changkat, a suburb and busy area of the Malay capital, Kuala Lumpur. The Changkat to which we were bound was tiny a *Kampong* (Malay Village) about twenty miles (32kms) south of Penang in the north-west of the Malay Peninsular. The particular feature that was of interest to us was, apart from having a very small collection of *atap* [27] dwellings, one doubling as a shop, it had some high ground in the form of a hill. The main hill that had the appearance of a large mound had yet another smaller hill atop of itself. An ideal place to sight a VHF radio and point the antennae in the direction of Medan, in Sumatra. Located not far from Medan, Indonesia's fourth largest city, was an AURI (Angkatan *Udara Republic Indonesia* -Indonesian Air Force) base equipped with a number of Soviet Tupelov Tu16KS twin-engine jet bombers (NATO designation *Badger B*). About 25 of these aircraft were delivered to Indonesia in 1961. This particular version, the KS, was equipped to carry Air-to-Surface missiles, namely the AS-1 or in NATO reporting language, the *Kennel*, its prime purpose being to destroy shipping. Being able to listen in to the operations of such aircraft had the possibility of gaining valuable intelligence on the aircraft's operating characteristics.

First though one must get to the top of the hill. Not easy, at least not for the Morris J2 being a two-wheel-drive vehicle. Under normal circumstances and in dry weather it would have been possible but this was the tropics and there had been a lot of rain in recent days. The track up to the summit of the main hill, wide enough only for one vehicle was, at this time, well covered in mud. The boss took one look at this and decided to turn around and return to Singapore. To myself, and I'm sure in the minds of others although they didn't voice it, after a 420 mile (676 Kms) journey in tropical heat, albeit with a night stop en-route, an about turn was not an option. Making my thoughts clear to our Flight Lieutenant I suggested that at least we should have a go. Our dear leader was not convinced but gathering a few of the keener types to unpack some bedding from the 3-ton Bedford I asked for a volunteer to drive the J2. Without hesitation, the quietest member of the team, Corporal Brian Sperrin, stepped forward. OK, we had a driver, so all we needed to do was to strap a good padding of bedding to the rear of the J2, to prevent damage to its rear door and do likewise to the front bumper of the Bedford. This done I climbed into the Bedford and proceeded to shove the J2 up the hill with much slipping and sliding and Brian's skilful handling of the steering wheel we made it to the top. Some of the crew followed in the Land Rover and I think the others walked. I don't remember anyone climbing aboard the Bedford or the J2 for the journey, "Oh ye of little faith".

One half of the space on top of the main hill was occupied by RAAF Personnel who operated a Radar that was used to fill a gap in the coverage required to afford early warning protection to RAAF Station Butterworth, some 19 miles to the north and close to the Island of Penang. This station was previously RAF but was handed over to the Australians in May 1958. Like ourselves, the Australians were living under canvas but that is where the similarity ended. Unlike ourselves, the Aussies were feeding on fresh food and meat every day and as one lad enviously reported, they even had steaks for breakfast. Their base Butterworth being but a few miles away they had no need to sacrifice any of their home comforts, not for them the routine of Composite Rations of which I will enlarge on shortly.

One of our larger tents was used as a dining facility and 'games' room. Not that there was much room for games other than those played on boards which were very popular with some. Competition was particularly fierce when the players of such games involved our operations officer, Peter Cousins. On these occasions some participants would get together and plan to beat Peter by fair means or foul, mostly foul. Peter knew this and would let us know that he knew but he always took it in good part.

The only other game in addition to the board games was darts and this was to have serious consequences for one young member of our team. A game in progress and John, no doubt with a thirst on, decided to get up from his seat and head for the bar, yes we had bar, of sorts. Being a tent there was no wall to hang the dartboard on so it was fixed on one of the substantial supporting poles. Just as John was close to this pole one of the darts players launched his missile. Normally this chap was quite skilled at the game but this time 'Sod's Law' intervened and he completely missed the dart board, the dart travelling on and hitting John in his left eye where it lodged as he fell to the floor. John was immediately rushed to the medical centre at Butterworth for treatment. At that particular time, if my memory serves me right there was a specialist eye surgeon visiting Penang and John was transferred there for further examination. He was soon returned to the unit but sadly he had lost the sight in that eye.

The only other time we had an occasion to do the A&E (Accident and Emergency) thing was when one of our number omitted to shake his jungle boots prior to donning them. There are, and no doubt always were many nasty biting insects in South East Asia and this time one had decided to lodge itself in one of this lad's boots. Whilst a scorpion sting can be very painful, fortunately this one was not deadly, not at least to a healthy male anyway. Another quick trip to Butterworth for a check-up and the victim was soon back at work.

Two minor injuries or ailments that fortunately did not necessitate a dash to Butterworth were quite common at Changkat. The first one was TPT, an abbreviation not found in medical dictionaries or common to medical students, but one that translates as Tent Peg Toe. Where there are a number of tents requiring guy ropes to secure them then there are tent pegs; they can be made of wood, heavy-duty plastic or steel, ours were of the latter material. Being in the tropics the flip-flop or flip-flap as some prefer to call them was a common and popular style of footwear but offered no protection when one was moving around in the dark and managed to find a protruding tent peg. Sometimes it may just have brought forward a loud ouch or more likely a somewhat stronger expletive. At other times though one could finish up with a cut or a badly damaged toe that required the attention of our medic. Some unfortunates were to occasion an attack of TPT when hastily en-route to the Elsan in the middle of night. That brings me on to what is more of an ailment than an injury often believed to be caused by a change of diet and known generally as a bad attack of the 'Trots' or Delhi Belly. With only one or two Elsans available it was a case of form an orderly queue. One colleague did tell me that he was so badly afflicted that at times he would complete his visit then immediately join the queue again. I don't remember either of these complaints affecting our operational capabilities however; such sterling stuff were the men of 54 Signals Unit made of.

We were not long at Changkat before a few of our number thought it would be a good idea to sample the wares on sale in the shop in the *Kampong* at the bottom of the hill. They were soon to find that the only commodity within this shop that tempted any of them to part with their cash were some small evil smelling black cheroots. These were a particular favourite of one member, one who normally rolled his own cigarettes. It seems that the cheroots, smelly though they were, came at a price more attractive than the DIY cigarettes that he was used to. A number of others, including myself did try them as a novelty but failed to get hooked. They remain forever in the memory of most of the original members of No. 54 Signals Unit and were tagged *'Changkaters'*, a name that was to stick.

I have learned from a contact living on the island of Penang that the hill at Changkat is no more, well, apart from a large lump of earth and quite probably even that too will soon disappear. It seems that the whole area is being developed for the production of palm oil. The hill may well have gone but we still have our memories.

Once the unit was fully equipped more detachments followed, many to various locations on the Malay Peninsular and to the Island of Labuan in North Borneo. There was also one to Sek Kong on Hong Kong's mainland more commonly referred to as the New Territories, a location already well familiar to myself and a couple of others. By the time we did this latter detachment we had taken on board a number of Special Operators (Telegraphy) with a Chinese language qualification. This trip to Hong Kong necessitated the use of seven aircraft. Among the types used were Blackburn Beverleys, at least one Handley Page Hastings and an Armstrong Whitworth Argosy. We made a brief stop at Saigon en-route where it was most interesting to see so much airborne and ground activity taking place. The war in Vietnam was still very much underway at this time.

Being fully equipped meant that we now had five short-wheelbase Land Rovers and trailers. Five long-wheelbase Land Rovers, four kitted out with radio receivers, both HF and VHF and Ferrograph tape recorders. One LWB was sometimes fitted with cryptographic equipment and a Collins KWM2 Wireless transmitter used to contact our base in Singapore where one of our 'straight' wireless operators remained. Confession time. Although I initially trained as a Telegraphist and had some amount of operational experience in sending Morse this was not a skill required of an intercept operator. I had not touched a Morse key since my days of operating as a Radio Amateur in Berlin and as many Telegraphists and Wireless Operators will know one can get the itch to actually handle a key when in the vicinity of one that is not being used. So with this KWM2 sitting there doing nothing late one evening in a remote location on the Malay Peninsular I decided to awake this lovely transmitter from its slumbers. Together with a like-minded colleague sitting in the rear of this well-equipped Land Rover tuned to the 20 meter band, hand on key, using a fictitious call-sign, I put out a CQ (all stations) call. The call sign I used (VK1...) indicated to any 'ham', at that time, wherever he may have been, that I was operating from Australian Antarctic Territory. Not surprisingly I was immediately inundated with amateur stations scrambling to have contact with me. I did actually reply to a couple saying I was on Heard Island in the Southern Ocean before I shut down. I now apologise to any 'ham' that may have thought he had a real prize contact on that night in 1965. I know, shame on me, I will now be refused membership of the RSGB (Radio Society of Great Britain). I was once a member but in my opinion they are much too elitist so I won't be applying anyway.

When en-route to the locations on the Malay Peninsular we always made a stop at the NAAFI warehouse in Johore where we filled one of the trailers, purposely kept empty until then, with duty-free beer. We had no problem keeping the beer cool when in situ, wherever it happened to be as we also towed two large diesel powered generators. In addition to supplying power to the radio equipment these generators also powered our large refrigerator and electric light bulbs in the tents. We may well have been camping but there was no point in being uncomfortable. In addition, one Land Rover towed a 600-gallon water bowser or tanker that was filled upon arrival on site. In many places the local water could be somewhat suspect and this is where our Nursing Attendant, Corporal Robert (Bob) Littlewood came into his own. In addition to attending to our needs in the way of minor accidents such as TPT and dispensing Kaolin and Morph for the trots or the *Larikan diris* (a corruption of the Indonesian words *Larikan diri* meaning to run or flee), a name often given to this affliction. Bob was also responsible for sterilising the drinking water. Once the bowser was filled with water, no matter from what source, be it the local village well or a garage in a nearby town Bob would have to test it then add the necessary amount of sterilising tablets to it. These tablets did not enhance the flavour but at least they made it safe to drink, something no one did until Bob gave the go-ahead.

Bob was another of those characters that one never forgets. Whilst the Special Operators would be busy doing what Spec Ops do the rest of the team did not always have tasks specific to their trade that took up all their time when on detachment,. The electrician would take care that all was well with the generators and the MT Sergeant would do routine maintenance on the vehicles. Others, such as the aerial riggers, the wireless fitters/mechanics and Bob, unless we encountered a problem or equipment needed attention they would have little to do and were allotted other tasks such as shopping trips to nearby towns or ensuring that any pools of stagnant water around the site had a liberal coating of diesel oil on them to prevent them being used as a mosquito breeding ground. In locations where very heavy rain was apt to flood our pitch it was all hands to the spades to dig drainage ditches. On one detachment to Gong Kedah in North East Malaya, Bob, on his first shopping trip called in to the village clinic and introduced himself on the basis that it is always good to have a friendly relationship with the staff manning such local facilities. One evening prior to us leaving Gong Kedah at the end of the detachment Bob approached me asking if he may donate some of the contents of his large first aid hamper to the clinic. As the contents of such hampers were always renewed on return to Singapore and the 'old' items disposed of I had no objection. He also asked if I would care to accompany him to the clinic that evening. As it was indeed a nice tropical evening, warm and with no wind, a normal Malay evening outside the monsoon season in fact, it was an invitation I was happy to accept.

On reaching the clinic the sister in charge and one of her nurses came down the steps to greet us with the words, "Good evening Doctor Littlewood" I thought, Bob you con artist but went along with the pretence, he had obviously built up a good relationship there, who was I to spoil it. It was also possible of course that the nursing staff had automatically assumed he was indeed a doctor. I was introduced as the Adjutant! On reflection I suppose this was an easy and uncomplicated was of saying to the nursing staff that his companion on that evening was the 2i/c of the unit. Anyway, a pleasant hour or two was spent in the clinic chatting with the staff who I think numbered only three or four, and sipping soft drinks, fresh fruit juice I think it was. The nightly Tiger would have to wait until we returned to the site. Another of Bob's responsibilities, which he took seriously was the maintenance of general hygiene on site. This unfortunately included the maintenance of the Elsan chemical toilets we used but as a conscientious member of his profession he took all this in his stride. Later, on a detachment to Labuan, North Borneo, not being enamoured with the practice of some twenty-five or so healthy males using the bushes as a urinal when the need arose, he introduced us to the Desert Lilly. [28] A row of five or six were sited tidily away from the accommodation and dining facilities, usually on the edge of the bushes or jungle, depending on where we were One other trailer in the convoy was always filled with 'Compo' ration boxes. These were cardboard cartons about 40 x 30 x 15 cm and filled with all sorts of edible 'goodies'. Well not always goodies as there were a variety of packs, from the basic to what could almost be called luxury. The latter type would possibly have a whole cooked chicken in a large tin but we were rarely to see any of these. Each pack was designed to feed one man for ten days or ten men for one day. This would account for them being officially titled, Ten Man Ration Packs but they were always known to those who ate from them as 'Compo'. Whoever designed the packaging labels on some of the items within these packs certainly had a whimsical turn of phrase. One item that I was rather partial to was a very thick round oatmeal biscuit that could simply be eaten as it was or soaked in milk or water to make a fair sized plate of porridge. The label on this item read, 'Ideal for munching on the march'. The exact words by the way. I suppose it adds to the phrase, 'An army marches on its stomach'. However, after eating two of these I would be more inclined to fall out and have a kip or put my feet up than to carry on marching, they really were quite filling. The other label which I shall never forget was with the tea and read something like, 'Makes a very nice cup of Sergeant Major's Tea'. Now there's a strange one. I know the Sergeant Major himself is different to everyone else and is feared and revered throughout his Regiment but, was the tea he drank so different? Come to think of it, if it was anything like the packs of dust that resembled tea only in its aroma then yes, his tea would have been different. Definitely not the best item in the carton. Among the more edible and the favourite of many were the tinned sausages, and the tinned steam puddings that came in two or three different varieties. The least favourites were the 'Hard Tack' biscuits, and the cheese. Each item alone had nothing going for it and when combined, as was often the practice to try to make the taste of one mask the other they still failed to please. The biscuit really lived up to its name and one risked damaging ones teeth on them. As for the cheese well, no idea if the milk it was made from came from a cow, a goat or a sheep but I very much doubt that it was from any of these. Perhaps its origins don't bear thinking about. The milk for one's tea was of the condensed variety and came in toothpaste type tube. Some of the lads enjoyed this in a sandwich, when bread was available from another source, or on biscuits, other than the hard tack I hasten to add..

In order that one could dine on some of the contents of these ration packs a small hexamine stove or cooker and matches were included. This cooker is a small disposable folding metal contraption approximately 12 x 12cm and when unfolded stands on four short legs. There is a compartment where one inserts the hexamine fuel tablet, sets light to it then places one's mess tin or other cooking utensil containing whatever one intended to heat up on top of the stove. [29]

Substantial, edible and sometimes even enjoyable Compo may be but like any other fare, after a short while becomes too much of the same thing. Therefore for dietary reasons and for the maintenance of good morale, a way to supplement this diet had to be found. Here I must admit, the authorities excelled themselves. When going on detachment away from base and where no catering facilities were available to us we took with us an amount of cash, always drawn from the pay accounts section by the officer in charge, had to be the commissioned officer of course, no knowing what the common other ranks would get up to with the cash. This officer kept the cash in a small safe in his tent (or more often for some reason, my tent) and each time we opened a box of Compo he would take an amount of cash from the safe and issue it to the cooks to enable them to go out and buy some fresh produce. This always went down well when they were able to purchase fresh vegetables and the occasional joint of meat or a number of chickens. On some of the detachments we, by arrangement with our cooperative leader would save up these allowances until the day before our departure to return to base in Singapore. The cooks would then go out and buy an amount of fresh meat and vegetables plus some wine. On that final evening we would arrange the trestle tables bedecked with sheets to resemble table cloths and dine in style out in the open These end of detachment celebratory meals were always an enjoyable affair.

Approximately two and a half years into the tour two replacement cooks arrived. Happily for us these two new fellows could work wonders with compo and always tackled, with enthusiasm, the job of feeding 20 - 30 hungry souls under difficult field conditions. One very nice innovative practice much appreciated by all was that on the day prior to departing Seletar, using the catering facilities in the airmen's mess kitchen, they would blanch a large amount of chipped potatoes and store them in a huge plastic sack. This meant that for the first meal on site at least , wherever it happened to be, there were always sufficient nicely deep-fried chips to go with whatever else they had conjured up.

Around the time of the arrival of the replacement cooks our first O.C. Flt Lt X returned to the UK and was replaced by yet another engineering officer. This time not an ex-ranker but a product of one of the elite Officer Training colleges. I really don't know what Flight Lieutenant Y expected to find when he arrived at No.54 Signals Unit to take over but I will lay odds that what he found was not what he expected. He was a thoroughly nice fellow and I found him fair in his dealings with the 'troops'. I know he enjoyed his sports, squash and rowing in particular and always seemed happy and relaxed to take part in these sports with the 'other ranks'. However, being a dyed in the wool member of the officer class he must have found it hard to come to terms with what he must have viewed as an undisciplined mob.

At the unit in Singapore we were all correctly attired, shoes polished and hair a respectable length but away from there, in remote locations dress was a case of anything goes. I like to think that, for my part, I ran the unit in a fairly relaxed manner, as long as the job was getting done, and getting well done, unnecessary bullshit was not on the agenda. Together, as a unit and not in earshot of outsiders, I used first names as an alternative to rank or surnames, after all most of us had worked, and at times, lived together for quite a while. This did not go down well with our new leader and he would, in the beginning insist on reminding me that this was not the way. I think that after a while he just gave up and let me get on with it. After all, things were running smoothly, there were no problems requiring disciplinary action and moral was, as far as I could tell, on a decent level. Sure, not everyone was keen on leaving their families and going off on detachment but it was a 'mobile' unit and that was how it had to be. I never heard anyone requesting a transfer on this or any other basis. One friend from those days tells me that on reflection he thought the unit was akin to the one featured in the TV series, 'It ain't half hot mum', in some ways I think he is right, it certainly was most unlike any other unit I had the pleasure to serve on.

Once again, but this time back at base in Singapore the folly of appointing non-experienced officers to command a unit such as ours came to light. By this time the new operations block had been completed and was fully operational when we were not on detachment away from base. In among the 'wheat' of the intercepts being taken down and transcribed there was, as is always the case, a certain amount of 'chaff' that was, after a perfunctory examination, of no great interest but was however, termed 'Classified Waste' that needed to be securely disposed of. In addition a fair amount of traffic that had been analysed and the results transmitted to our RAAF colleagues in Perth or to DSB in Melbourne via CK2, had also to be destroyed. The safest way to achieve this aim was simply to burn it, easier said than done when there is no incinerator available. There may well have been an incinerator of sorts on the station (RAF Seletar) but to transport such classified waste to a facility that would have been operated by local native labour would have been too much of security risk. Our new gallant leader became aware of this but considered that we did not need an incinerator at all, he had a solution. So, he had this 'solution' installed in the toilet block. One of those small machines fastened to the wall that ladies use to destroy their used 'towels'. When we all finally stopped falling about laughing one of the lads decided to feed said machine with a few sheets of paper. We then, very roughly, worked out that it would take at least one month to destroy one week's classified waste by this method but the thing would probably go into overload and burst into flames long before that.

New boy finally convinced he submitted a request for an incinerator to be built in our compound. With usual Chinese diligence this building was soon completed and quite a large affair it turned out to be. A brick construction the size of two Land Rovers side by side, a large steel flap on the top, rather like a top loading washing machine the whole being topped by a large chimney and immediately dubbed 'The Mosque'. All went well with this new toy until one day the lads on the burning detail were caught out by a sudden tropical downpour of the like one only sees in the East. Unfortunately, a fair amount of rain entered via the open top flap before it could be shut with the inevitable result that some of the paper already in the incinerator was more than slightly dampened. Not to be outdone the two lads involved, after a short pause and no sign of any further showers, added some more dry waste and put light to it. The fire initially took hold but then the damp paper took over and simply produced a large amount of smoke from the chimney, a bit like the ceremony for choosing a Pope really. Perhaps it could have been used to choose a C.O that knew what life in the sigint world was all about. The two likely lads then decided that the only solution would be to feed in some more classified material but this time with the addition of a liberal amount of petrol, chuck a lighted match into the lower air vent where normally the ash would be raked out, making sure the top door was closed and stand well back. This procedure was duly and eagerly carried out and was followed by an almighty explosion; the steel door was too heavy to be moved by this but a large amount of our semi-burnt secret waste shot out of the top of the chimney. By this time most other personnel on the unit, being alerted by the very loud bang had gathered to view a display of partly charred paper high in the sky, eventually coming to rest outside the compound. Oh Dear! I think was the initial reaction of most chaps but that changed to something else when they were informed that they would now have to exit the unit, spread out and search the surrounding areas for every scrap of our charred secrets. Following this incident, much to the surprise of many, no instructions were issued regarding the use of petrol, the safety 'elf was yet to make his presence known in that part of the world. However, a quantity of wire mesh was fitted to the chimney top to prevent any recurrence of partially destroyed classified material making like it was bonfire night.

The spot where we camped at Gong Kedah (sometimes spelt and pronounced Kedak), was an old, deserted but still usable airfield of sorts and had some decent buildings in situ. Among these there was a fairly large open-sided building suitable for use as a dining area, by the look of its configuration this had been what it had originally been used for. Trestle tables and folding chairs installed it became almost homely. In the evening it would be used for social activities such as card playing and enjoying a beer. No one was any longer keen on playing darts following the unfortunate accident at Changkat.

One evening, not being a card player myself, not that I have anything against it, it's just that I'm not very good at it, I and one other of similar persuasion took a Land Rover and sought out what appeared to be a sort of coffee shop in a nearby local *Kampong*. Here, sitting on the only space available, the floor, we were welcomed by the occupants and offered a drink of something that may or may not have been coffee, which we politely accepted. Conversation was difficult. Although our Malay was of a fair standard these folk spoke a dialect that I believe was more akin to an Indonesian dialect spoken in Sumatra. There was a small table in the centre of the room that was covered with what looked like tiny damsons still on the remnants of branches and twigs of whatever tree they came off. We were invited to try these, which we did, and immediately we bit into the fruit our mouths became incredibly dry, almost paralysed, whereupon the locals fell about laughing at our predicament. I don't know if they could eat this fruit, I didn't see any sign of this; maybe they just made some choice brew from it, perhaps that is what we were drinking. After we had been chatting for a short time and conversation became easier, one chap told us that there was an ex-RAF Flight Sergeant living in the next *Kampong*. This fellow had apparently stayed behind after WWII, maybe he was an ex-POW of the Japanese or maybe he had escaped from the Japanese and they had hidden him, its anyone's guess, they either could not or would not say more. When we indicated that we would go and pay this fellow a visit, we were told in no uncertain terms that he did not, ever, want any visitors, particularly from a world in which he no longer had any interest whatsoever. In effect it seems the locals had really taken to him, possibly he had gone native, married a local girl, and they were the guardians of his privacy. We were happy to respect this and took the matter no further.

On leaving this, doubtful, coffee shop, and with the blessing of the occupants we took with us a few of the smaller branches that held the small purple fruit with its strange dehydrating powers. The guys back at the site will love these - not, we thought. So, arriving back and joyously presenting branches and fruit to the still card playing gathering with the words something like, "hey, you should try these, they are delicious". Once they did just that the result was predictable, branches and fruits were hurled in our direction as we headed hurriedly to our tents. They did the hurling in silence as their mouths did not seem to be in a fully functional mode.

As the reader will by now be aware, not all sigint collection is carried out from ground based stations, interception of signals traffic is also carried out on both sea and airborne platforms. In the period between May 1965 and May 1967 I logged a total of 155 hours in the air, most of it over Indonesian territory gathering intelligence. For a greater period of this time I was accompanied by a fellow Indonesian language trained operator, Euan McKinnon, a Scot from the Isle of Skye, one of the best friends I ever had and now sadly no longer with us. On only one other occasion was this friend and colleague absent and that was on a trip to Hong Kong when one of the Chinese language trained operators came along. The platform for these flights was a De Havilland Comet2, formerly a British Airways passenger aircraft suitably fitted out for its intelligence gathering role. This aircraft would come out to Singapore with a team of ELINT [30] operators who were tasked with intercepting and recording signals from the Indonesian Radars.

Before we could take part in these airborne activities we would of course require the appropriate quantity of flying clothing and accessories. Having obtained the necessary document duly signed by our dear leader we headed to the store responsible for issuing such items. As many ex-service readers will know, personnel employed in stores guard all the equipment in their charge as though it were actually their own and always seem reluctant to part with anything without argument. So, it was with some trepidation we entered the building and presented our 'demand' I think this was the title of the document, we were too polite to actually demand, anything. The request for each of us was, one Suit Flying tropical, one Mae West type survival vest, one flying helmet together with oxygen mask, one 'bone dome' or outer, hard flying helmet and one Aircrew Flying Log Book. We had first paid a visit to the medical centre or sick quarters to have our heads measured for the bone dome. Also requested was a canvas brief case, commonly known as a Nav Bag to be used to transport whatever documents we needed. To our surprise, the stores fellow issued everything without comment. We had at least expected the question, 'what do you fellows want flying kit for, you are not aircrew?' We were later to discover that written on the 'demand' quoting the authority for such issues were the words, 'Sigs Plan 13' It would seem that instructions, possibly from MOD, had been communicated to all the stores on the base that, should this magic number be quoted on a 'demand', any items listed on the document were to be issued without question. It did however, backfire on one occasion when our MT Sergeant requested a pallet upon which to store the vehicles spare wheels. Land Rovers normally carried these items on the bonnet, but not a good idea when the vehicles were at times, left unattended outside the base where the spare wheels could easily be removed and quickly spirited away. The MT sergeant consulted a catalogue that had many pictures of such pallets and picked out one he thought would do the job. When the pallet arrived on a large vehicle it was absolutely massive, far larger than anything needed for storing Land Rover wheels. It was actually a pallet for storing large aircraft wheels but, Sigs Plan 13 dictated that no questions were to be asked so that is what we received, red faces all round, well at least for the MT Sergeant.

On the day, or night of the scheduled flight my colleague and I would journey from our base at Seletar and drive to Changi (now Singapore's large and very busy international airport) where we would attend a briefing regarding the flight route, receive a list of frequencies on which we could expect to hear military transmissions of interest, this list being typed on rice paper. It didn't actually say on this paper, "if captured by the enemy eat this" but that is obviously what was implied. We would then deposit our personal belongings, wallets etc in a safe but retain a certain amount of cash, don our flying suits place our identity discs around our necks and board the bus to the aircraft.

At this time Indonesian airspace was a strictly no-go area but no one seemed particularly perturbed about this as we would be flying at around forty two thousand feet. Not that the Indonesians were without the means to reach us at that height, they had more than forty of what were in those days, a so-called new generation Soviet aircraft the MiG-21 (NATO name *Fishbed*). We had either adapted an 'it can't happen to me' attitude or had our doubts about the operational capabilities of the users of such hardware outside the Soviet Union. Either way it was a chance that our dear leaders seemed happy for us to take.

There was as far as I can recall only one occasion when fighter aircraft were believed to have been 'scrambled' against us, this was by a number of L29 *Delfin* (Dolphin -NATO name *Maya*) aircraft of which the AURI had recently taken delivery. This Czech built aircraft was, and no doubt still is somewhere in the world, primarily a Jet fighter training aircraft with a service ceiling or operational height of a little over 36,000 feet and we were probably long gone by the time they reached anything like this altitude.

There was however, one flight or sortie that gave us some rather exciting moments to say the least. Prior to this flight when we would normally have been attending the briefing, the two Spec Ops, my colleague Euan and myself, were told to go and have a coke or something we would not need to attend the briefing. We did think this was rather strange but enjoyed another soft drink before take off. About an hour into the flight I was excitedly nudged by Euan who was writing frantically in his log, (we sat side-by-side). One glance at his log (I was monitoring a different frequency) had me both reaching for the supervisors call button and wondering how long it would be before 'lights out'. Euan's log read "have you fired your missile yet", and the next line, "yes, it is speeding on its way to the target". The supervisor, a Flight Lieutenant, took the log but didn't seem to be overly worried, in fact he smiled and looked very pleased. Of course, he had been at the briefing and knew full well what was taking place in nearby airspace and in the ocean some forty odd thousand feet below. I have never quite been able to work out why we were not kept in the picture. Perhaps someone thought that our reaction would not be as immediate as it was if we had known exactly what we were logging. Euan and I, now happy that we were still sitting comfortably and not either trying to stay afloat in the ocean, or worse. We continued to monitor a number of relevant frequencies for some time with our efforts producing some further intercepts related to what had just been logged. It was later revealed to us that the target of the missile or missiles was a small uninhabited island.

About ten days prior to this flight some of our number were informed that they would be going to sea on board HMS Oberon, a submarine of the Royal Navy. I don't believe that they were told what the mission was until they put to sea and to this day I am unsure as to where their underwater travels took them. They were away for about six weeks and at least two of their number were sporting the makings of fine beards when they returned. I did at first think that as this took place at around the same time as the missile tests were taking place. That the two missions may have been connected on the basis that they may have been beneath the ocean at the time that we thought we were about to be blasted out of the sky. I entertained the thought that they would be monitoring, at periscope depth, similar signals traffic emanating from surface craft. Maybe also, someone on board the sub' was observing a small uninhabited island that was about to be completely destroyed by a Kennel missile or missiles fired from TU-16 Bombers. Unfortunately, as the 54 SU operators on board the submarine were those with a Chinese language qualification and they were away much longer than was necessary for this 'one-off' exercise I have to discount this theory. Unless of course the uninhabited island was in Chinese waters! I must presume that whoever planned this sortie of ours must have had information that this Indonesian 'exercise' was scheduled. Such information must have been gained either by Humint [31] or intercepted signals traffic, Sigint, or both.

Landing, on this occasion at Labuan, I found that a vehicle was parked at the aircraft's steps waiting to speed me to a hut together with our logs of all intercepts appertaining to the missile firing. It seems that the folk down in Melbourne were anxious to get their hands on this intelligence without delay. In the hut a very kind Australian Officer (I think he was army) sat me down at a table with a typewriter already loaded with the paper required for me transcribe the details of our logs. He then brought me an ice-cold beer that I promptly spilt when I whacked the typewriter carriage back. Oh hum, he brought me another. Lovely fellow, can't see an RAF Officer waiting on a Flight Sergeant like that, he would probably detail one of his minions to do it. All in all, probably the most exciting flight of my life.

During one of these flights Euan decided to sample the rice paper in case we ever did have to eat it. He reported that the paper was OK but he didn't like the ink! He had a great appetite. As such flights were usually of between four and five hours duration and we often returned at times when all the service catering facilities had shut up shop we were given a substantial lunch box to take on board. On one occasion, having sat on board for about an hour waiting to take-off, the pangs of hunger started to attack my colleague so he opened his cardboard box, devoured the large chicken leg, the chocolate, the bread roll and butter, the apple and whatever else was in there, finishing with an appreciative belch then deposited the chicken bones back in the box. Imagine our surprise when just minutes after finishing this gourmet snack it was announced over the intercom that because of a technical fault the flight was to be aborted. Descending the steps, lunch boxes in hand complete with, in all cases but one, the unconsumed contents, we espied a sergeant wearing the familiar white attire of a chef, hand outstretched to receive back his goods, he hoped. When it was Euan's turn to hand over his box, which he did dead pan, and without a word, the reaction of the chef was a joy to behold. When he took this particular box in hand it was obvious to him that it did not even approach the weight of the other boxes he had so far received and handed to his assistant to place in a vehicle. First of all his mouth opened as if to say something but no sound came out, then he shook the box, not once but a number of times finally opening it to reveal some very bare chicken bones and a used paper napkin. I was next to hand over my box (I had eaten only the chocolate) but had to wait. The chef still had the almost empty box in hand and he was not looking in my direction but with mouth still open and eyes wide, his gaze was on Euan's back as he made for the crew bus, priceless!

Following these flights and on the occasions that we returned to Singapore, which was most of the time, we would first of all go to CK2 for a de-brief and to hand in our logs in order for the content to be transmitted to RAAF Pearce in Western Australia and to DSD Melbourne. During one of these de-briefs whilst I was still a Sergeant I had a most pleasant surprise when our operations officer, Peter walked in, having specially made the journey from our base at Seletar. He approached the desk at which I was sitting and told me to stand up which I did wondering what the hell was going on. Peter then held out his hand, for me to shake and said, "Congratulations, Flight Sergeant". My promotion to Chief Technician had been promulgated but I was never to wear the badge of rank appropriate to that as, at the same time, I had been promoted to Acting Flight Sergeant (paid). This in effect made me the NCO i/c the unit, a big shock for the Chief Technician in that post at the time. Peter told me he wanted to be the first to congratulate me as our Flight Lieutenant OC, Flt.Lt X at this time, when receiving notice of this promotion did not want to accept or confirm same. Purely it seemed because of the effect it would have on the present incumbent filling the post of NCO i/c the unit. Peter, quite rightly I am pleased to say, thought otherwise and told the Flight Lieutenant he couldn't withhold the promotion without reasonable grounds that of course he did not have. A short time following this, all unit Commanding Officers were asked to submit the names of any NCOs they considered suitable potential officer material. Our OC submitted the names of the other two Senior NCO Spec Ops. Some time later when we were all chatting this OC, said to me in front of the other two, "I didn't put you forward because you are a bit of a rough diamond". This remark was possibly not meant as a compliment but that's how I took it. I think our OC had not forgotten the time when arriving at Changkat and I, contrary to what he, as the boss, wanted, pushed the J2 up the hill. If my behaviour on that day was considered to be in the style of a 'rough diamond' then I was, and still am, happy with it. I would like to conclude this paragraph on a better note but unfortunately for my two SNCO colleagues their recommendations for commissions were not successful.

The aforementioned flights took up only a small portion of my time and the detachments throughout the area went on apace. On one detachment to Labuan (North Borneo) camped on what had been a Japanese landing strip during WWII, with the bomb craters made by Allied bombing still in evidence we were to receive feed-back on some of the encrypted material we had intercepted. Whilst during confrontation Indonesian diplomatic signals traffic may well have been employing high grade ciphers their armed forces in the field were not. We learned early on via our Australian counterparts that the Indonesian military units were relying on a Hagelin machine to encrypt and de-crypt their traffic. The Hagelin in use was a mechanical machine about the size of a small commercial typewriter and was readily available on the open market. As we did not have such a machine in the field our intercepted cipher traffic was forwarded, by various means depending on where we were operating, to our Commonwealth colleagues either in Labuan (North Borneo), at Pearce in Western Australia or at CK2 in Singapore. We had up until now not very often received any feed back as to what most of these encrypted messages did contain but as at such times we were operating in support of the Commander Operations Borneo we lived in hope that it was put to use. We were however, from time-to-time informed of the contents of some intercepts and often in rapid time. On one occasion when the 'enemy' had scored an own goal the response to our submitted encrypted traffic was immediate. Obviously someone was interested in any follow-up traffic we may have been able to supply in relation to this incident.

An Indonesian Artillery unit located at *Long Bawang* a small airstrip in *Kalimantan* (Indonesian Borneo) just a few miles from the Sarawak border mistakenly took a pot shot at one of their own C-130, Hercules transport aircraft. Unfortunately for them this aircraft was carrying members of the RPKAD (*Resimen Para Komando Angkatan Darat*) an elite army parachute regiment. Their shots were on target and the aircraft crashed at the airfield and subsequently caught fire. Our intercepts did not tell us whether or not there were casualties but later reports say that the troops did manage to parachute out and the crew walked away from the wreckage. Some of the follow-up intercepted traffic was quite interesting. Apparently and understandably the Lieutenant in charge of this artillery battery was not the flavour of the month and subsequent intercepts told us he had rather hurriedly been posted elsewhere. Possibly for his own safety I should think.

As previously mentioned the Indonesian and Malay languages, apart from a small number of differences are practically one and the same. I was sometimes asked how we knew that we were in fact listening to Indonesian and not Malay. With the Morse code intercepts it was not always immediately apparent but the procedures used, to which we would have been familiar, would soon give us a reliable indication. The voice intercepts could usually be quickly identified to the source by the use of certain words. As an example the Malay for the numeral nine is *'lapan'* whereas an Indonesian would say *'di-lapan'*. The biggest giveaway however was at the end of a transmission when the station sending would invite the receiving station to transmit. A Malay would, in my experience, always use the word commonly used throughout the English speaking world, 'Over'. Not so the Indonesian who would say *'Ganti'*, (lit. To change).

In view of the amount of contact we were to have with our Australian counterparts at RAAF Pearce it was decided that a liaison visit by some of us would be useful. As it happened two of us almost did not make this visit.

This liaison party was made up of Dave Shanahan, Dennis Hall, Peter Cousins and myself and we were booked on RNZAF (Royal New

Zealand Air Force) flight from Changi. We were billeted in the transit hotel at Changi overnight for an early morning start the next day. Dave and I in one room, Peter and Dennis in another. Early calls were booked and it seemed that the other two responded to theirs but Dave and I just carried on sleeping. Until that is I awoke with a start when I realised the time. Quickly waking Dave we dressed and then set out on a run into Changi Village hoping to find a taxi. Luckily for us we quickly found a large Mercedes taxi with its Chinese driver fast asleep. It was, after all very early in the morning. Flashing a fistful of dollar notes and piling into the taxi we were quickly on our way to the airstrip where we could see a RNZAF Handley Page Hastings taxiing for take-off. No sooner had we entered the reception building than the NCO clerk had picked up the phone and was asking the Control Tower to contact the aircraft and ask the pilot if he "Could take two late starters from Seletar". What a fine obliging fellow that pilot must have been to have accepted such a request. We were then piled into a vehicle and rushed out to the aircraft where, as soon as the doors opened we were jointly hoisted and pushed up into the aircraft where we could see our two colleagues smiling at our predicament. Strapping ourselves into seats we were quickly airborne and were offered a coffee by a smiling female Loadmaster. What a wonderful airline!

As it was forbidden to use Indonesian air-space at that time we had first to fly north around the top end of Sumatra then south to re-fuel on the West island in the Cocos Keeling group in the Indian Ocean 2750kms north-west of Perth. These islands have been under Australian administration since 1955 and are now a popular tourist destination. During our short stop-over there in March 1965 I saw no evidence of this so I must assume it was yet to be 'discovered'. There was a fair sized building catering for transit passengers where we enjoyed a meal before spending some time on a beautiful beach before continuing on our way to Perth.

We were to experience a pleasant two weeks at RAAF Base Pearce, 35kms north of Perth. The buildings in which we were to liaise with RAAF personnel analysing intercepted traffic were a collection of wooden huts. Because of the warm climate and lack of air-conditioning the windows of such huts were always kept open and any conversations taking place inside could easily be heard by anyone in the surrounds. As there always seemed to be a gardener or workman in the vicinity steps had to be taken to prevent such workers eavesdropping, either accidentally or otherwise. This was achieved by having a radio, tuned to a popular broadcasting station switched on at medium to high volume all day long. As it happened the 'Seekers' had just hit the charts with their latest number, 'There will never be another you' and consequently this seemed to be played more often than anything else. A pleasant enough number sung by Judith Durham if my memory serves me right. Weekends were free for us to do as we liked. I don't know what my colleagues got up to one Saturday morning but I found myself breakfasting alone, apart from RAAF NCOs that is. At the breakfast table chatting to a couple of these fellows I was asked what I intended to do that particular day. As I really had no idea it was suggested that I go down to the main beach not very far away and watch the annual international surfing championships. Good idea I thought but I just had to ask, 'What happens if there is no surf?'. When this pair had stopped laughing I was informed that. "There is always surf". So I took myself off to watch these championships. I spent most of the day there gazing at a sea that looked more like a mill pond with a large number of would be competitors aimlessly wandering around the beach. Always surf indeed. I was never to see those two fellows again whilst there which is probably just as well. They would probably accuse me of putting the hex on their championships by daring to enquire about the surf, or lack of.

Our return to Singapore on 24th March was by an Air India Boeing 707, a pleasant flight made all the more so by having the company of a number of professional entertainers as, apart from one star-struck female, the only other occupants of the economy cabin. The entertainers were a well-liked (at least in Australia) English singer by the name of Mark Wynter (now an actor) and a popular Manchester band at that time, Freddie and the Dreamers. Freddie Garrity and his companions that made up the band had just completed a successful tour of Australia and were returning to the UK. Cilla Black was also on board but as she was in the first-class cabin we were not to have the pleasure of her company. 'The Dreamers' were certainly very good company and we spent a fair amount of the time chatting and having a few laughs with them, one of them, I think it was Pete Birrell even helped himself to a couple of chips from my meal.

While still waiting for our new building work to be completed and in order to keep some of the operators suitably occupied when not on detachment they were sometimes loaned to the joint GCHQ/DSD station, CK2 a few miles down the road from Seletar. They were seated alongside some of the civilian GCHQ operators employed there and doing exactly the same job but for a lot less pay. I was surprised to learn that the civilian operators were not required to pay UK Income Tax whilst so employed in Singapore. Not being happy with this situation but also fearing that I would not be able to do much about it, I nevertheless penned a letter to the UK Inland Revenue simply asking why. The answer I was to receive was typical of what we came to expect from the mandarins who sit on their fat backsides in the UK. It was something like. "You are in the, the UK Civil Servants are not". I was more than happy when the building work was completed and we could keep our operators on home soil as it were and no longer lend them out.

By early 1966 the undeclared war termed *Konfrontasi* had all but ended. One would think therefore that it was then time for our unit to pack up and go home. This was not to be however. Although the normal overseas tour for RAF personnel was of two years and six months duration the original six operators had, prior to 1966, been asked if they would extend their tour by eighteen months. Five of us were happy to do this and one, for personal reasons, extended for a slightly lesser period. The 'war' may well have been over but there was still an opportunity to remain in situ and gather intelligence in the S E Asian theatre and at the same time keep the 'troops' active. To this end we would sometimes enlist the help of two of the helicopter equipped squadrons on the airfield.

The squadron flying the Bristol Belvedere Twin-rotor helicopter, No.66 Squadron was the one we used most and I must say they seemed happy to help now that their operational commitments were no longer as demanding as they were when the conflict was at it's height. Most of us would board the aircraft but I never remember either of our officers taking an active part. Once airborne we would fly to some quiet location and abseil down a long rope using only hands and feet, mostly feet, to control our descent to the ground below. We were always dressed for the occasion and armed with our rifles to add an air of reality to the exercise. I was usually first down on the basis, 'if I can do it so can you'. The others quickly followed but I don't think all enjoyed the experience. One lad in particular froze halfway down the rope still a considerable distance from *Terra Firma*. With the helicopter wanting to get away and he not able to re-ascend there was nothing else for him to do but simply let go. He did and fell to the ground, fortunately for him the *Terra* was not so *Firma*, the ground was very wet and soggy and he suffered nothing more serious than acute embarrassment and a sore ankle. This latter incident took place using a Westland Whirlwind aircraft from 103 Squadron which also seemed happy to help us exercise and have fun in the sun.

On a number of other occasions we would take part, as 'umpires' during large Joint RAF/Army exercises but would not be doing any actual umpiring. Normal practice for umpires is to display white crosses on the vehicles and for personnel taking part to wear white arm bands. We were happy to go along with this requirement as it gave us an air of neutrality. As in all large exercises of this nature there are always Friends and Foe, a 'Blue' Army and one of another colour but neither of these opposing forces were aware that we were still keeping our hand in and monitoring their communications therefore they did not always take care about what they were saying on the air. On such an exercise near the small town of Titi in the state of Negri Sembilan on the Malay

Peninsular we camped alongside a tiny strip of grass land, a suitable landing place for the Scottish Aviation Pioneer, a single engine STOL (Short take-off and Landing) aircraft. The pilot of one of these aircraft circling above us and in communication with his 'Army' was heard to say "They are wearing white arm bands but beware." It looked very much like someone out there didn't trust us.

Sometimes such aircraft would land and the crews pay us a visit where we were happy enough to offer them refreshment and which they were happy to accept be it tea, coffee or a beer, the latter from our large well-stocked refrigerator.

Here I must introduce another of our 'characters' one Bernard David Snell. David's first passion was, and I believe probably still is aircraft and anything to do with aviation in general. On this occasion at Titi he was wandering around with a tape recorder recording the sounds going on around us, in particular the occasional aircraft that came and went. Thus, whilst practising his hobby we had a flying visit from a fairly high ranking RAF officer who alighted from his aircraft and approached David, who was wearing a tropical flying suit not his usual Khaki drill uniform and enquired, "are you from the Farnborough noise monitoring team?", David, hardly pausing in his fiddling with his tape recorder replied, with his usual panache, "No sir, I'm SAC Snell from 54 Signals Unit". Said officer made no further comment, he must have taken it for granted that the 'Spooks' as we came to be known did all sorts of strange things. More about David later but first a few words about Titi.

During the quiet periods here, particularly when there was no aircraft activity I was pleased to take in the view, a pleasant and tranquil scene that sometimes featured a few happy smiling Malay children. Then I would start to think and reflect what life must have been like there just a couple of decades ago during the Japanese occupation when such places were the scene of terrible and evil brutality. Many thousands of innocent Chinese were brutally murdered, butchered to death. In the state of Negeri Sembilan alone the number of Chinese massacred is estimated at least four thousand mainly unarmed innocent working men, women and children. Titi, where I now sat enjoying a cold beer, was the location of the single largest massacre of mainly innocent Chinese civilians by the Japanese during WWII. One thousand four hundred and seventy four souls were killed in one afternoon. [32] How easy it is to forget that such horrors ever took place when relaxed and surrounded by comrades and friends.

As it was not always deemed possible to find an ideal place to site the units vehicles and tented accommodation consideration had to be given to the time when we would have little more than a jungle clearing to set up in. One of the main difficulties would be the locating of antennae. Dave Snell, being keen to experiment with antennae came forward with a suggestion that might just work and he designed one that came to be known as the 'Dustbin'. This took the form of two cardboard cylinders one above the other and covered in aluminium cooking foil. The feed connector was via TV type 300-ohm cable, the lightest such cable available at the time.

So with the dustbin built back at base, a small team comprised of David, Fred Muir the Corporal Aerial rigger, Alan Pinder the Wireless Fitter and myself set off for a number of different locations on the Malay Peninsular to test it out using a hydrogen filled meteorological balloon to raise the dustbin to a decent height. The first location was in the open at the Jungle Survival School in Johore. It seemed apparent on the very first test that a feeder cable of the type used was maybe too heavy for the job as instead of having the dustbin in the vertical plane as hoped it remained almost horizontal. As there was a fairly heavy wind blowing at the time we thought maybe this was at least partially to blame. We therefore reserved final judgement for the next location which was to be more sheltered and among trees.

Whilst at the Jungle Survival School I stayed in the Sergeants' Mess so was not able to attend breakfast with the rest of the team. However, when we got together later for the trials one of them came to me and mentioned an incident at breakfast. One of the three when holding his bacon, sausage, and beans laden plate out for eggs was asked by the chef, "how many eggs, one or two", "Three please" replied this hungry fellow. I never did work out why so many 54 SU members had such healthy appetites.

The next location for the dustbin test was much further north and although adjacent to a small army camp was among the trees. Sadly, even though there was only a light wind the antenna and feeder cable remained virtually horizontal in the trees, this obviously didn't help so we reached the verdict that the too heavy feeder cable was mainly to blame and we would have to go back to the drawing board. Apart from the lack of success it was an enjoyable few days out to see yet other parts of the peninsular.

Another exercise in which we were to take part involved the RAF Regiment, the 'soldiers' of the Royal Air Force. We set up camp in a fairly remote area on the Malay Peninsular surrounded by jungle and a unit of the Regiment did similar just a short distance away but within sight of our pitch. They were a good bunch of guys to exercise with but I can't give them credit for thinking that we were a bunch of no-hopers when they tried to play daft tricks on us. One late afternoon their young officer came across and asked if some of us would mind going over to them and help look for a bayonet lost in the undergrowth. There were certainly enough of them to do the searching in not a large area so it was obvious they were up to something. Anyway we decided to go along with whatever it was and followed the young fellow most cautiously. It turned out that it was just as well we were cautious but it did rather spoil their fun. Just at the perimeter of their pitch one of our party spotted what looked like a long slim tent peg, where there should not have been any such thing. Further investigation revealed a very fine wire leading to yet another peg device, obviously a trip-wire, nice one RAF Regiment but it didn't work. Letting 'Rupert' know we had seen this trap one of us gave the wire a tug with the foot just to see what had been planned and sure enough there was a brilliant flash accompanied by a loud bang further along the line. That put paid to their silly tricks but they were yet still to try to out-fox us in an ambush situation.

This was more like it, playing soldiers again, I was loving it. The Regiment guys went off to hole up somewhere along one of the many jungle roads along which we, armed with blank ammunition and smoke grenades were to drive three Land Rovers. The idea being of course that they were to catch us unaware and ambush us. I went in the lead vehicle with a driver and the other two vehicles were spaced out to the rear. All went well until we came to a small wooden bridge over a stream and something was telling me that this could be the place. So halting the convoy I dismounted and signalled to Dave Snell who was in the second vehicle to join me. The plan was for the two of us to walk slowly across the bridge with the vehicles following close behind. About two thirds of the way across the bridge I noticed to my left what I at first thought was a large piece of cotton-waste that had maybe been thrown there by the driver of one of timber carrying lorries that would sometimes pass along such tracks. Then it dawned on me, not cotton waste but a scrim net or camouflage scarf of which there had to be a face behind. Obviously this guy or guys were waiting until we had at least one vehicle at the end of the bridge then he would open fire. Foiled again. Quietly whispering to Dave to be ready to throw a smoke grenade in the direction of the scrim, hit the deck and open fire. With a scream from me of, 'enemy left' whilst hurling my grenade, we both went to ground and opened fire. All hell was then let loose, as the hopeful ambushers opened fire with a Gimpi (General Purpose Machine Gun) into the clouds of smoke. As far as I was concerned, it was too late, the volleys from both Dave and myself would have put this fellow out of action well before he could have squeezed the trigger. At the de-brief later when we got together I was to meet the young lad of scrim scarf fame who admitted that he had been cursing the Flight Sergeant (me) who had put paid to his moment of glory. So it was a triumphal party that arrived back to regale those who had not been on the exercise with tales of our success. One exercise that, on reflection whilst downing my can of Tiger, I thoroughly enjoyed. That evening the boss told me that during his chat with the Squadron Leader in charge of the Regiment contingent in Singapore and who had accompanied this party had told him that if his Flight Sergeant ever wanted a job with the RAF Regiment he had one. Comments well appreciated but too late, about 15 years too late, Sir! All this love of 'soldiering' in my case didn't mean that I would react the same if faced with real live action and being shot at. I don't think anyone can say in advance how they would act in such cases, I certainly can't. All I can say is that because of my enthusiasm I would, at least, know both how to handle and have confidence in whatever equipment and arms I was supplied with.

Back at Seletar I had joined a branch of the British Sub-Aqua Club. Although located on this RAF Station its members, in addition to RAF personnel, were from the Royal Navy and British Army stationed on the island. Although I had done a fair amount of snorkel diving in Australia I had never been able to do any real diving using an aqualung. Here I had the opportunity to put that to rights and trained in the station swimming pool one evening per week and went on open water dives in the sea off Singapore most Sundays when not away from base. It was not long before the committee members suggested that I should join them. After some persuasion I reluctantly agreed and finished up as chairman becoming quite involved in the activities of the club.

In the RAF there was, and maybe still is, a scheme known as Expedition Training where organised teams could be partially or wholly funded by the RAF to take part in expeditions such as mountaineering, trekking or exploration either on land or under water. It was obviously the latter that the Sub-Aqua club was interested in and an expedition was planned to Pulau Tioman a small island in the South China Sea some 35 nautical miles off the east coast of the Malay Peninsular. This involved a fair amount of planning before the details could be submitted to the officer in charge of expedition training. Such expeditions are not always approved and it was with some trepidation that myself and a couple of other members formally approached this officer with details of what we had planned. Initially the meeting did not go too well as the proposed expedition involved hiring at least one boat of undetermined sea worthiness to get us to our destination from Singapore together with its Chinese owner as crew. One member of the club, a UK civilian employed by the RAF, something to do with building maintenance or Works and Bricks as it was known to us. This chap had a fairly reliable boat that he was willing to take along. Then we came to who would be the responsible person in charge of this expedition. Myself being little more than a novice diver had no ambitions in this direction and I had made that clear to the other committee members. One member at least was very well qualified and had been diving for a good many years in a number of locations throughout the world, he was the obvious choice. He was Sergeant so he did carry some authority but this did not impress the officer who would decide whether or not this proposed expedition got off the ground. The finger was then pointed in my direction, me being the senior ranking member of the club even though way down in the pecking order when it came to sub-aqua activities. Eventually following further discussion concerning the boat hire approval was granted providing that I was willing to lead the expedition, I was lumbered.

Pulau Tioman was a most beautiful island, I say was because when we took the expedition there it was inhabited by a small number of Malays and I believe one white lady (I think Australian and who lived in the interior). I recently looked at Tioman on the internet and certainly received a shock. It now has Chalets, Hotels and even a landing strip. Pulau Tioman is only about 40km in length and 12km wide. During my time there I was aware that there were a small number of *kampongs* or villages in other parts of the island but we were never to visit them. There was one close to the beach where we pitched our tents but apart from meeting the village Headman and a few others on our arrival we only ever saw one of the sarong attired, young ladies when she came to fetch fresh water from a source close to the beach. We would also occasionally catch a glimpse of the charcoal burner as he attended to his fire about 50 metres in from the water source.

The day long journey by boat from Singapore to Tioman was uneventful but the actual arrival in the dark gave us some cause for concern. The smaller boat owned by the UK civilian was the faster of the two we used, the other, a native fishing boat, hired in Singapore being the larger was crewed by a Chinese Singaporean and was the one on which most the team including myself travelled. Upon our arrival in the bay on the eastern side of the island the smaller boat was already anchored and those on board were able to ascertain the depth of water, information we would need to know to avoid running our larger vessel aground. Luckily, as it happened, the owner of the small boat was an ex-RAF wireless operator and he signalled to me in Morse by a hand-held torch with the message that I remember quite clearly to this day, "Come right in". We did just that but when we arrived alongside we found that he was actually sinking, slowly but surely. This caused something of a flap as in the lower part of the cabin of the small boat was the small JAP engine we were to use to power the lights in the tents. Not that we could not have operated without such modern lighting but the generator was one I had borrowed from the unit and I did not really want to be the one responsible for writing it off by submersing it in the South China Sea. The generator and other items, stored in the lower half of the boat were quickly removed and transferred to our vessel. After all this time I no longer remember where the leak was but following some hurried baling out of a fair amount of water it was soon plugged, so panic over.

We spent the rest of the night on board and awoke at daybreak to see a beautiful white beach against a background of palm trees. We were quickly to learn from one team member, a film buff, that this was one of the beaches that were featured as Bali Hai in the 1958 film South Pacific. I recently learned also, courtesy Wikipedia, that the 1970s Time magazine selected Tioman as one of the world's most beautiful islands, following my short stay there I have no argument with that whatsoever.

We were also able to see a small party of natives standing on the beach looking in our direction and presumed one of them to be the Headman of the village. We quickly inflated the large rubber dinghy, once part of the equipment carried in bomber aircraft and a party of us rowed ashore. I must say, being the only Malay speaker in the party, I felt a bit like one of the latter day explorers stepping ashore to parley with the natives. Initially the local party seemed more curious than anything and also somewhat hesitant but once they realised that one of these 'invaders' spoke their language it was all smiles and friendly greetings. Pleasant chitchat over I then asked the Headman (yes we had presumed right) for permission to pitch camp on his beautiful domain. Permission graciously granted we conveyed our grateful thanks and paddled back to the boats to bring our equipment ashore and get to work erecting the tents and sort out where everything was to be stored. We were not to see any of that greeting party again except for a few small boys who would appear from time to time, curious to see what we were up to and later, when the diving started they would, sometimes out of natural curiosity, want to see what we had gathered from the sea.

As expected, the sea around the island was teeming with life, shoals of small fish, individual species many beautifully coloured among the equally colourful coral, all nice to look at but better left alone. Some members of the team, unlike myself, had a large amount of in-depth knowledge regarding the variety of seashells and underwater life to be found there. This was just as well because I was quickly to learn which particular specimens one could handle without fear of suffering a possible fatal bite or sting. I no longer remember the names of all the shells to be found there but among them were large Helmet Shells, named because they looked like, and some were approaching the size of, the traditional fireman's helmet. There were also a variety of Cowrie shells some of them beautifully patterned, Augers that were a sharp pointed cone shaped shell, a particular species found in the area and in Indonesian waters I learned one had to be most wary of if handling. There were many Conch shells in a variety of colours and patterns.

On one particular dive when a number of divers were in the water and I was sat on the side of the boat about to enter the water one diver surfaced, looked at me and shouted, "come on, hurry up, there is a shark down here". So thinking, 'well if it's OK for him and the others down there, it must be OK for me' and in the water I went. There indeed was a shark there, probably about two to three metres in length circling the group of divers I was about to join and did. No one appeared to be panicking but all were keeping an eye on the sharks movements which thankfully were not showing any outward signs of aggression, After a few more circuits of its potential breakfast it must have decided that we did not look tasty enough and quickly departed the area. The only other sighting of sharks I had whilst there was a number of recently born dead ones that had been washed up on the beach.

The sea in the area around Tioman has a large amount of detritus and wreckage left over from WWII, both British and Japanese including the British battleships HMS Repulse and HMS Prince of Wales, both sunk by Japanese aircraft in December 1941 with a great loss of life when attempting to intercept Japanese landings on the east coast of Malaya. In Singapore I did write to the British authorities, on behalf of the Sub-Aqua club for permission to dive on the wrecks of these two vessels but permission was refused as both vessels were regarded as war graves. [33]

In the second week of our stay on the island we were surprised by a visit from the Royal Navy's aircraft carrier HMS Hermes that anchored some way offshore. A number of the crew and some Royal Marines lowering a boat came ashore a short way along the beach from where we were and proceeded to have a swim and a barbecue. Apparently, according to our RN members, this is quite normal practice in the Royal Navy when the opportunity presents itself. As what fresh food we had brought with us had been consumed in the first few days of the expedition and we had since been living on compo one of our naval types thought this was a good opportunity to go on a scrounging mission. A number of us swam out to the smaller boat and then headed out to the carrier. As soon as we were alongside a head appeared over the rails of the carrier that did seem a hell of a height above us. Without hesitation our RN fellow shouted for the officer of the watch. A short pause and requested officer appeared asking first what we wanted, the quickly shouted reply was, "Have you any bread?" With that the officer of the watch asked where we were from and on receiving the reply, 'Singapore' disappeared. Within a very short space of time he reappeared and shouted, 'catch' at the same time throwing down a very long slender loaf of bread to the waiting hands of our communicator. Five or six more loaves were to follow whereupon we shouted our grateful thanks and headed back to the beach to enjoy some delightful fresh bread with our next meal. Thank you Royal Navy.

The time came for us to leave this paradise island but not entirely empty-handed. There were a good number of what appeared to be very old fossilised clamshells in the waters around Tioman. We were aware that the maritime museum in Singapore had one such shell reputed to be 2000 years old and some of what we were seeing, according to the museum's regular visitors among us, could be much older. The club had previously donated a Remora fish to the museum following one of our Sunday dives around Singapore. In the past a variety of other specimens had been donated but that was before I joined the club so I had no knowledge of these apart from the being told that the museum was always grateful to receive them. Following a certain amount of discussion it was decided that they might just like another giant fossilised clamshell. This specimen really was quite large, three to four feet in diameter and very heavy, taking three of the strongest members to bring it to the surface and a further number to heave it on board the large boat. We were later informed that this shell was 4000 years old. A worthwhile effort.

The return trip to Singapore and reality went almost without incident. As it involved an overnight journey most of us on the larger vessel decided to get our heads down and catch some sleep en-route. I chose the hatch that covered the engine compartment, a nice warm place to bed down. However, as the night went on it became even warmer, unnaturally warm in fact. Summoning the Chinese boat owner we raised the hatch to be treated to the unwelcome sight of a not insignificant amount of flames reaching upwards towards our position at the open hatchway. It was obvious that something was well alight in the vicinity of the engine. With typical Chinese nonchalance, almost as if a fire in this part of the boat was a regular occurrence (maybe it was), this fellow entered the compartment and quickly extinguished the blaze leaving me to wonder just how close we may have been to disaster.

December 1967 brought me close to the end of my tour in S E Asia and on the morning of 31st December I received a pleasant surprise when the Station Commander's driver arrived at the door of my married quarter in Seletar. When I opened the door I was handed an envelope, that, when opened revealed a letter informing me that I had been awarded the British Empire Medal in the 1968 New Years Honours List.

7 TREACHERY

Prior to the end of an overseas tour one was asked to choose an area in the UK to where one would prefer to be posted. Most people, if they had strong ties with a particular area, would quite naturally choose that area. One had to submit a choice of three areas but there was no guarantee of being granted any of the three chosen areas as often the end result depended on operational requirements.

My relief and replacements for the other four remaining operators had arrived in Singapore and it was time for me to submit my choice of postings. I think my first choice was RAF Wyton in Cambridgeshire, not that I had any personal ties there but at that time it was the home of the Squadron that was the user of the Comet aircraft that I had enjoyed some time aboard. I was not expecting to be employed in an airborne role there that was in the main, performed by linguists of another flavour. I knew however, that there was a certain amount of analysis work to be done at Wyton by chair-borne special operators. RAF North Luffenham in Rutland was my second choice as the school had since moved there from Digby. I no longer remember what my third choice was but it was certainly not Digby. Unfortunately, much to my disappointment, that is what I got to the eventual detriment of my career as a Special Operator. Operational requirements seemed to be the reason or someone thought I had enjoyed too much of a good time in South East Asia and that it was time I joined others at number 399SU. Not a bad place to work, it was simply all the extraneous bullshit that went with serving on a large operational station that I was not looking forward to.

On returning to the UK one was always granted a period of disembarkation leave. The period of this leave was determined in the ratio of one days leave for each month served overseas. As I had completed a longer than usual tour I was entitled to and granted a longer than usual period of leave. I was able to add some of my annual leave entitlement to this with the result that I was not due to report to

Digby until mid May 1968.

I spent a fair period of this leave as a van driver working for a company that supplied ladies' hairdressers with the products they needed to ply their trade. This meant that most days of the week I was driving around Leeds, Bradford and surrounding areas in West Yorkshire including the seaside resort of Scarborough delivering packages. I enjoyed this break from service life, driving around in the fine spring weather where, in many of the establishments I visited, the young ladies commented on my four-year tan. They would ask "and where have you been on holiday?" Little did they know whilst I was happy with my overseas tour it was hardly a holiday. After a few weeks as a delivery boy I received a telegram from my younger sister in Manchester giving me the sad news that my father had died and asking me to return home. It was indeed a sad day when we buried my father, a soldier of the Great War 1914-1918 who saw action and was wounded on the Somme just three weeks prior to his seventeenth birthday.

So it was with not much enthusiasm that I arrived at Digby in May 1968 and was initially employed in the traffic analysis section at No.399 Signals Unit. What I at first dreaded was 'morning prayers' the session each day attended by the commanding officer and other hangers on. This was the daily meeting where they expected to be briefed on the current situation in relation to Soviet air force movements, in particular their intrusion flights into European air space other than their own. An easy enough job for anyone that had been working in this theatre for a time and some compatriots had done little else. However, I drew the short straw here and together with the Warrant Officer in the Traffic Analysis section had to do the daily presentation. As I had been in the South East Asia zone for four years and did not have much of clue on the current European situation. I quickly had to bone up on this to prevent myself looking like a right dummy. With the help of colleagues I soon got the picture.

Not long after settling into this new routine my two former SNCO colleagues from our time in S E Asia and myself were selected to attend a course of training in Prisoner Handling and Questioning Techniques at the Joint Services Intelligence School, Templer Barracks, Ashford in Kent. After the shock of Digby and all that it entailed this was a welcome diversion. On arrival at this school, we were surprised to learn that the other students on this course were all commissioned officers, mostly from the British Army. There were also two RAFVR (Royal Air Force Volunteer Reserve) officers and one RCN (Royal Canadian Navy) Captain. This latter officer threw the school staff into a bit of a panic when they heard the word Captain in relation to a naval officer, a very high rank indeed in the Navy. They all relaxed however, when they realised that all ranks in the Canadian Armed Forces were equated to Canadian Army ranks. Therefore, our RCN captain was no different than a captain in the British Army or a Flight Lieutenant in the RAF. We enjoyed the course that was very well organised with the practical elements having a realistic feel to them. At one stage we split into teams of four, one of the team interrogating a 'prisoner' in a 'bugged' cell while the other three listened in in a separate room. The idea being for the three to criticise and comment on the effort made by their colleague in the cell. We were also to experience a made up language known as Gobbledegook in use on part of the course and. It certainly lived up to its name but thankfully we were not expected to make any sense of it until two words cropped up that we were well familiar with. Both words were taken from the Malay language and it was obvious that the staff there did not know their meaning believing that they were indeed part of the Gobbledegook vocabulary. On hearing these two particular words the three of us had to chuckle. Someone in the past had obviously slipped them into the vocabulary of this 'pretend' language with tongue in cheek. The words themselves were; *Bukit Puki*. *Bukit* is simply a hill but *Puki* is a coarse or abusive Malay name for the female genitals.

The chief instructor on the course was a Major who was formerly the Commanding Officer of the interrogation centre in Aden during some of the time the British were stationed there. So three RAF NCOs left Ashford as trained interrogators, although none of them ever had to use skills they acquired there. The course was over all too soon and it was back to Digby and more surprises.

I was soon to learn that my beloved 54 Signals Unit where I had spent possibly the best four years of my service time was to be returned to the UK and disbanded. Being disappointed with the decision to break up such a successful unit I sat down and put pen to paper listing a good number of reasons why this should not happen and further suggested a plan for future employment of the unit in the UK and Europe. I submitted my suggestions that covered a good number of A4 pages, to the SIO (Senior Intelligence Officer) who would have been my line manager. A couple of days later my 'manuscript' was unceremoniously deposited on my desk by the aforementioned SIO, with the words, "it won't happen' and off he strode. A few short months later the unit did indeed return to the UK and was not disbanded but was employed in exactly the manner I had suggested. I wonder how big a pat on the back the SIO received for my efforts! No 54 Signals Unit was indeed disbanded some years later but as I write I learn that it was reformed at Digby in October 2014. I would have hoped that on such an occasion this unit would have been granted a Unit Badge/Crest that reflected its South East Asian origins but that did not happen. I learn that it will display the badge of the Second Tactical Air Force (2nd TAF) which is the badge it was offered when it first requested individual recognition some years previously when being deployed to Germany. The badge will of course have the words, 54 Signals Unit emblazoned upon it but I think that is a poor substitute for a badge giving recognition of the unit's history. [34] In order for me to get to grips with the situation at Digby it was necessary for me to spend some time at the sharp end, this as the supervisor in charge of the set or operations room where between twenty and thirty operators sat in front of radio receivers tasked with intercepting a variety of foreign communications. I sat at a desk at the entrance to this room and my two assistants, both with the rank of Chief Technician, were at desks spaced down the room.

The shift pattern we were working at the time to cover a 24 hour period meant that within the pattern one would work the morning shift, have the afternoon free then be back on watch that evening. Not a pattern enjoyed by all but it did mean that within the cycle one had a 'stand down' or two and a half days off. Following the stand down one would be expected to report for duty on the afternoon shift. As at all watch change over times the three senior NCOs would receive a quick briefing from their opposite numbers who were going off duty regarding the current situation and any unusual events or intercepts that had taken place during their watch. With the handover completed and all the operators seemingly occupied it was normal for me to have a few words with the other two senior NCOs and often the conversation would be sprinkled with social chat such as what one got up to during the stand down. On one such occasion, chatting with the Chief Technician seated nearest to my position, Dougie as he was known to all, mentioned that he had driven up to London on one of his days off and during the journey, he thought, in fact he was sure, he had been followed by someone on a motor cycle. We and the rest of the world were soon to learn that he had indeed been followed and subsequent shattering revelations were soon to follow.

It would have been just a couple of hours into the watch on the morning of 11 September 1968, only days after Dougie had told me of the event in which he thought he was being tailed when two gents in civilian clothes were shown into the set room by the Warrant Officer in Charge of operations that day. These two suited fellows complete with 'pork pie' style head gear were obviously, to me at least, SIB (RAF Police Special Investigation Branch), that particular style of hat seemed to be de rigueur for the 'Branch' in those days and was always a give-away as were the Minis they drove around in that featured twin fuel tanks. Standing one either side of Dougie they confirmed his identity and without any further ado escorted him from the room. I was later to learn that he was taken to an office along the corridor normally used by the Warrant Officer Administration and interviewed by a Special Branch Police Officer from Scotland Yard before being taken to his married quarter where he lived with his wife and family. His married quarter and his car were then searched in his presence and a large amount of spying paraphernalia was discovered. Among such items were a camera disguised as a cigarette case and a number of OTPs (one time pads).

Naturally, all the watch were puzzled by Dougie's unscheduled and abnormal departure but no one seemed to know anything further and anyone that was in the picture was not saying anything. All was revealed that evening however when one operator, doing what was strictly forbidden, was listening to the BBC evening news bulletin. This lad let out a shout and said, "Bloody Hell! Dougie Britten has appeared at the Old Bailey charged with spying". In normal circumstances I would have had to place this operator on a charge, he was being paid to monitor foreign transmissions, not listen to the BBC. However, in the excitement, any thought of disciplinary action was forgotten and his misdemeanour had the result of telling all present what they were waiting to hear regarding Dougie's unexpected disappearance.

In the days following these events RAF Digby was awash not only with members of the press but with SIB and the same Scotland Yard Special Branch Officer that had initially interviewed Dougie was often to be seen arriving in the 399SU car park. Myself and a number of others were interviewed more than once; it would seem the hierarchy at Digby were in a panic in case Dougie had a successor-in-waiting.

Ronald Douglas Britten, to give him his full title, was 'recruited' by the Soviets in London in 1962, if we are to believe the contents of the statement he made following his arrest. Whilst visiting the Science Museum he states that he was approached by a Russian calling himself Yuri. and was asked if he could obtain a handbook for the T1154 transmitter. This was the transmitter that together with the R1155 radio receiver was installed in practically all RAF Bomber aircraft during World War II and later in the 1950s was still being used on RAF Air-Sea Rescue craft. In addition, in the 1950s many were later gifted to and installed in the premises of ATC (Air Training Corps) Squadrons for cadet training purposes. The T1154 was not on any 'Secret' or classified list and I doubt that it ever had been on such a list. So many bomber aircraft with this equipment on board were 'lost' over enemy territory during the war that details of same would have been well known both to the enemy and other advancing armies who at that time were our allies. Since the end of the war it had been possible to purchase these transmitters among others in the usual outlets that sold Army/RAF surplus equipment. The main buyers of such being Radio Amateurs or Hams as they are generally known and of which Douglas Britten was one, operating with the call sign G3KFL.

If this is indeed what happened, Britten must have thought it a trifle strange, to be approached in such a manner particularly as the approach was made with the Russian addressing him by his amateur radio operator's call sign by way of introduction. At the same time he must have known that the handbook being asked for did not warrant a security classification and therefore no harm could come of it. The correct procedure to adopt however, following such a meeting would have been to report same to his superiors but we know this is not the course of action he chose to take. A short time after this alleged approach he was posted to Cyprus, the Soviets being aware of the sigint units on the Island must have been rubbing their hands with glee at this.

Once in Cyprus he treacherously supplied sigint information to the Soviets. In addition to wanting all that he was able to supply, his handlers wanted, or rather demanded, all manner of information from him. Could he give them names of other likely 'recruits'? Did he know of individuals on his unit who had a weakness for women or were having affairs? Were any of his colleagues addicted to drink? Were there any homosexuals? Indeed all manner of personal information that could leave a person open to blackmail. Continuing to receive payment for any information he was able to supply, such payments no doubt being used to advance his lifestyle and assist in the purchase of his Volvo car that he was buying on hire purchase. He was obviously encouraged to do as he was asked and accordingly he supplied names of likely candidates. By now therefore he was betraying his colleagues for cash, unforgivable, particularly unforgivable as I have reason to suspect that my name would possibly have been one that he passed or rather later sold to the Soviets, not in Cyprus but later in the UK in 1968.

Chief Technician Douglas Ronald Britten was born in Northampton on the 31st October 1931 and joined the Royal Air Force 18 years later. In 1953 whilst serving as a Corporal at RAF Station Habbaniya in Iraq he married Megan George, herself also a serving member of the RAF.[35]

He returned to the UK in 1966 and was posted to No. 399 Signals Unit at RAF Station Digby for the second time in his career. It was here that he was arrested on the11th of September 1968 and charged under the Official Secrets Act 1911 with passing secrets to a foreign power. On 4 November he appeared before Lord Chief Justice Lord Parker at the Old Bailey, much of his trial being held in camera. He pleaded guilty and was sentenced to serve 21 years in prison.

Following his arrest there was obviously much discussion among his former colleagues including myself regarding events leading up to his arrest. Was he really recruited after someone had fingered him as a potential source of classified information? Or, for some reason did he himself volunteer his services? Personally I was unable to contribute very much during such conversations as, although I knew of Douglas Britten I never actually met him until I arrived at Digby in May 1968. A good number of the others however had known and served with him for some years, both at Digby and during his overseas postings. When discussions came around to 'if he was indeed fingered, why', and for what reason? The general opinion of some of these colleagues who knew him well was that he was not a womaniser and some regarded him as a family man although it was thought by others that his marriage was a little on the 'rocky' side at times. He had three daughters, the first being born in 1954 in Lincolnshire as was the second in 1955. The third child was born in Cyprus in 1958; this was during his first tour of duty on that Mediterranean Island. What reasons could a potential informant give to the Soviets to suggest that Douglas Britten might be of some use to them? He was certainly not a homosexual nor was he in any extra martial relationship. He was however, known to be often short of cash and was on a number of occasions in debt to the NAAFI for purchases he had made. Back at Digby in 1967 a number of cheques that he cashed in the Sergeants' Mess were not met. A local garage also contacted his unit commander after a cheque in the sum of eleven pounds also bounced. He received a number of warnings on these matters and after it came to light that he had borrowed money from a Junior Rank he was charged and appeared before the Station Commander where he received a severe reprimand. [36] Did he volunteer himself; perhaps by visiting or contacting the Soviet Consul, if so, then no doubt the motivation for this would have been his financial situation. I am not suggesting that this is what happened but taking into account what we now know of his financial situation it was certainly a possibility. In his statement he claims to have received only £700 - £800 for the vast amount of information he had supplied to the Soviets.[37] Apart from his expensive brand new Volvo car he was also the owner of some expensive amateur radio equipment. I realise that he had his salary from the RAF but if we include any extra overseas allowance it still would not have been a great deal to provide for a family of five which included himself and enable him to afford these items. So, if he was being economical with the truth on that matter I would suggest that he was not telling the truth and the whole truth about his meeting with Yuri that was to give the impression that the Soviets targeted him rather than him offering his services. The first question that comes to mind is, how the hell did Yuri know that Britten was going to be in the Science Museum that day? This could have come about perhaps because he mentioned it in a conversation with another radio amateur in a transmission that was monitored, or perhaps in conversation with a 'Ham' in the eastern Bloc, possible, taking into account the amount of political influence affecting amateur radio there at that time but I very much doubt it. In those days one could not operate independently as a radio amateur in that part of the world, one had to be a member of a club that was run on political lines. In this way the 'party' would be aware of who was contacting who and would certainly pick up on any communication with persons in the West that may be of use to them at some future date. These are of course my personal thoughts on the situation and I know of no strong evidence to support them.

Some time after his release, having served about 13 years of his sentence, he took up employment with British Rail as Relief Crossing Keeper on the Level Crossing at Skewbridge Lincoln where on 30 January 1990 he died following a heart attack. [37] At the time of his death at the age of 58 he was living at No. 40 Bargate Lincoln, a freehold terraced property in a tidy but not the most salubrious area of the City.

I would dearly like to have had a chance to speak with Mr Britten prior to his demise as I firmly believe that he had sold my name to the Soviets as a likely candidate for recruitment. The reason he would have considered this so are as follows. In March 1968 following my return to the UK my marriage had broken up and I was living in what was considered to be an extra marital relationship with a lady that already had two children. As I was also paying maintenance to my wife from whom I was separated, and not being exactly 'well off' I would have seemed a likely target for exploitation. Initially, although my cohabiting was frowned upon and could have resulted in me losing my security clearance no action was taken and I carried on working with sensitive material for a good number of months. Eventually however, someone, possibly under pressure from a higher authority, panicked, fearing I might be approached and I was transferred into another trade group where I would have no access to any secrets whatsoever. The rate of pay was less, the work mundane and following the most interesting, and at times, adventurous career I had previously enjoyed, very boring. Although I was not due to leave the RAF until my fifty fifth birthday still some 15 years in the future, having completed more than the qualifying time for pension I submitted my application for discharge. I could well have soldiered on, even in my new situation boring at times though it was if it had not been for the constant attentions of the SIB.

One particular incident left me in no doubt as to where my future lay following my return from two weeks leave that I had spent in Germany. On this occasion one Friday afternoon two of the SIB Muppets paid me another visit. They did their usual questioning act for a couple of hours and even searched my room in the Sergeants' Mess. If I hadn't have been so fed up with all their questioning and their superior attitude it would have been laughable. These two clowns really thought they were on to something when they espied a short-wave radio receiver on my sideboard. A string of moronic questions followed, but they were not satisfied with the answers I gave. One of the two left my room to make a telephone call and returned with an officer who they believed knew 'all about radios'. Pointing to my radio they asked him one question, "can one send as well as receive messages on that". The officer, with a large grin on his face, looking at me replied, "of course not, it's a receiver". That satisfied them but what the idiots did not realise was that a receiver was all that a spy needed to receive his instructions, for his replies he could use dead letter drops and other well known means of secretive communication. It seemed that someone somewhere was determined to find another mole and in the absence of anyone else I would be the subject for investigation. In fairness I did hear later that at least one of my former colleagues and possibly others had had similar treatment from the SIB.

At this time I was stationed a good many miles from home and I drove home that evening with pains in my chest, obviously brought on by the stress of that afternoon. During that weekend at home I decided that enough was enough and on my return to work on Monday submitted my application for discharge to pension.

What did not help me and in fact must have given weight to the authority's reasons for their keenness to point their dirty finger in my direction was the extraneous duty I had been allotted whilst at Digby. Most officers and Senior NCOs can find themselves lumbered with such duties that have nothing to do with their normal day-to-day responsibilities or employment. They can be put in nominal charge of any of the clubs or activities on the station. It doesn't mean that they have to take part in any of the activities of such clubs but to ensure that they are kept in a tidy state prior to any inspection or more importantly, that they are indeed being run or operated in the manner for which their title suggests. For example, that the Chess Club was being run as such and giving it such a title was not just a cover name for a boozing or gambling den. Unfortunately, as a former amateur radio enthusiast someone must have thought I was the ideal person to be in charge of the station's amateur radio club. Disaster! It was in that particular club that Britten was to tune in to his Soviet masters and receive some of his instructions. I don't remember going in to the 'Ham' club more than a couple of times and then it was only to check on its state prior to a routine inspection of certain areas of the station by the Station Commander. Why could I have not drawn the Badminton club or the Philatelic club, both being activities I was familiar with, then maybe the dreaded SIB would not have jumped on me quite so eagerly.

It was this series of events that led to the beginning of the end of my career in the world of sigint. Leaving aside the unpleasantness and upheaval of those last few months that left a bad taste because of the treachery of a colleague I am left with so many happy memories. I greatly enjoyed most of my time in the RAF and more particularly my time in sigint. I met lots of interesting people, made a few friendships, some that have lasted to this day. I even spent a short time in the company of one of the 20th century's most infamous spies and had another of the same ilk as a colleague. I never for one moment imagined or anticipated the events and rewards that would follow when on that day in June 1948, as a sixteen year old, I raised my right hand to swear allegiance to King George VI, his heirs and successors. I was to travel to places I had only previously heard of and was, in my leisure time, humbled and privileged to tread the earth in the footsteps of those soldiers that had so bravely died in the defence of Hong Kong. I was to experience the sights, sounds and smells of the East and was fortunate to have the benefit of receiving an education not to be found in any classroom.

EPILOGUE

The demise of my career in sigint was to start with an unscheduled trip to our fair capital city. Reporting for duty one morning at my desk in the traffic analysis section, I found a small handwritten note on a scrap of paper that read something like, Report to New Scotland Yard (it gave details of which entrance to use) tomorrow at (time). Civilian Clothes. The (time) train from Lincoln St. Leonard's would be a good one. Signed………SIO. No name just the title of his appointment.

This spineless creep, signing himself SIO (Senior Intelligence Officer), the same one that had unceremoniously rejected my suggestions for re-forming No. 54 SU, had not the grace to summon me to his office to tell me this, instead he kept well out of the way. The miserable shit even tried to make out he was helping me by giving me what he reckoned was a suitable train time. Why should I travel to Lincoln some 12.5 miles (19km) distant when there was a even more suitable train leaving from Sleaford just 8.5 miles (14km) down the road from Digby and just about 5 miles (8km) from where I was living at the time. Needless to say I ignored his 'helpful' suggestion and took the train from Sleaford.

I entered the Scotland Yard building by side entrance and after identifying myself to a lady receptionist was handed a slip of paper in the form of a pass and given verbal instructions as to which room upstairs I was to report. I expected an office but it was more like a ballroom, huge the only furniture being a trestle table and chairs at the far end. At the table sat two very young RAF Police Officers of the commissioned variety. Introductions over they opened a file that contained my service record that they started to quote from. What a pair of prats, "you have had in interesting career, been all over the place" said one. "I see you were stationed at Goch" said the other. It was then I gave up hope, Goch, just over the Dutch border into Germany, I spent no more than two or three nights there in transit I was never actually stationed there. These two Ruperts were just going through the motions. They continued with the nonsensical small talk before saying that because of my marital state and the risk it posed I could no longer be employed on sensitive duties. They then offered me a choice; return to Digby but report to No.591 Signals Unit. To be employed at this unit did not require a high security clearance and although it had close cooperation with GCHQ, doing some domestic monitoring it did not handle material particularly useful to a foreign power. The option to this was to re-muster to the trade of RAF Admin. This being the trade where all the drill instructors, some small arms instructors, firing range supervisors, keepers of discipline and good order and the like came from. I was then told that I had no time to make up my mind, I had to decide there and then. By this time I was so pissed off with the whole business that I chose the latter option. This pair of comedians then made it clear that my entrance to No.399 Signals Unit when I returned would no longer be possible, except to clear my desk.

Reporting to 399 Signals Unit the next day to clear my desk I found that someone had already had a go at this and helped themselves to some documents I had in my drawer. Not classified documents but a couple of copies of a Government White Paper that I had personally purchased relating to Regina v Ronald Douglas Britten. Then, without any further delay I was posted to RAF Swinderby in Lincolnshire to await the start of the next Senior Administration course.

The Scotland Yard performance left no doubt in my mind that, once Britten's interrogators had learnt that my name was among those that he had given, or rather sold, to the Soviets panic set in. I can just imagine someone grabbing the phone and calling the Commanding Officer of RAF Digby, and screaming "get rid of him, sharpish, we don't want another bloody potential spy on our hands" Or, maybe they were beginning to think they already had one but were finding it difficult to find any evidence.

As it was to be some weeks before the start of the Admin course I was given a few mundane tasks on the station, which at the time was

No. 7 School of Recruit Training. I assisted the Flight Sergeant in charge of the Orderly Room with a few minor clerical tasks, took statements from recruits on behalf of and sitting alongside a Corporal Policeman who, having broken his arm was unable to write them himself and finally was put in charge of the Guard Room with a Sergeant and a General Duties airman as assistants. The Guard Room, was the reception area where visitors would be required to report when entering the station. Formerly the province of the RAF Police, having a number of cells for holding miscreants awaiting transfer to larger penal establishments but this was no longer the case. Then came my claim to fame; The SWO, the Regimental Sergeant Major of the Royal Air Force, was unexpectedly and hurriedly posted, on detachment to RAF Changi in Singapore to assist in its imminent closure. This now left a very important gap on the station and I, moving into the holy of holy, the SWO's office, was the one to fill it.

At the time I was in charge of the Guard Room another SNCO, a sergeant arrived on station saying he was also being re-mustered into the admin trade group. I asked him what trade he was, "Engines" was his reply. To me this simply meant he was an aircraft engine fitter or mechanic, fine but why on earth would anyone from this trade be re-mustered to the General Duties Administrative trade group? The knowledge he required to carry out his calling could hardly be described as sensitive unless that is he had been working on some top secret piece of kit and was considered unreliable. I am aware that a small number of airmen in the 'Technical' trades did sometimes apply to re-muster to the Admin trade group. In such cases it was because of a positive lack of promotion prospects in their trade. That did not, in this case ring true as this particular tradesman was already a sergeant with possibilities of further advancement within his trade. As he didn't quiz me about my reasons for being in this situation I respected his silence, although I did think it strange but left it at that. He had been allocated a married quarter on the station upon his arrival and had an attractive German wife. As it happens my partner was also German! Something the SIB would have taken into account when selecting this particular NCO for 'undercover work'. Of course he didn't quiz me, he already knew everything about me. Although I couldn't believe my own thoughts at the time, things did start to fall into place. He spent a fair amount of time with me, on and off duty making sure we were in each other's company, with wives/partners at any function we attended. The ladies seemed to get on rather well, I had not conveyed my suspicions to my partner and I don't know if the Sergeant's wife was aware of the real reason for her husband's sudden detachment. I was living on a farm some distance away from the camp, unmarried couples were not of course allocated married quarters. On at least one occasion I invited this fellow and his wife across to the farm for dinner. In retrospect I think he, with the possible innocent cooperation of his spouse engineered the invite. When the Admin course started, himself and wife disappeared as suddenly as they had arrived. I had been entertaining a snoop, an RAF policeman in disguise. That was just the start of me realising that I was not going to be left alone and at times would continue to be hounded.

The Senior Administration Course of six months duration was a prerequisite for Sergeants in the Admin trade aspiring to the rank of Flight Sergeant. As I was already of this rank my arrival into the trade didn't go down too well with the other students who immediately saw at least one Flight Sergeant vacancy that they would have hoped to fill had already been filled. One other sergeant candidate on the course was a former Royal Marine, whom I had known for many years and who was a good friend that I was most pleased to see among the, mainly hostile, gathering. Of the other course members there were only two or three other really bright lads who took my arrival in their stride and simply wanted to get on and obtain a good pass mark. Apart from all the bawling and shouting on the parade square there was a fair amount of service knowledge, including RAF Law, a thorough knowledge of Queens Regulations and Air Council Instructions and various other procedures relating to disciplinary matters to be digested and tested on. It was on these latter subjects that at least three failed the course, so they said goodbye to any further chance of promotion anyway. I must say that apart from some of the ceremonial drill procedures that I had never before experienced I found the course a walk in the park and came top with close on a 100% mark. Not what some of the morons wanted or expected and throughout the course had tried to put obstacles in my path to make me look stupid. The particular Sergeant who took us through our paces on the drill square and who was charged with teaching us all the none-too-often used ceremonial procedures such as those performed at military funerals was a particularly obnoxious character. He was coming to the end of his career and no doubt hoping to make it to the Flight Sergeant rank before this happened therefore boosting his pension. To him I represented an obstacle in his path and his obvious dislike of myself never faltered, poor sod.

A short time after I had re-mustered the pay structure in the RAF underwent a dramatic change. It became, basically, that one was to be paid not entirely for what one did but for what one might be expected to do. Personnel in an 'Advanced' trade that included Special Operators of both categories, Telegraphy and Voice were to receive a higher rate of pay than those in merely 'Skilled' trades and RAF Admin fell into this latter slot. So, apart from having the SIB on my back not only had I taken a drop in pay but eventually my pension would be based on the lower rate of pay. Douglas Britten had done me no favours at all.

I continued to receive further visits from the SIB who, going by their pattern of questioning were convinced that there was a successor to Britten, maybe something else he had said during questioning had made them suspect this. One line they always took with me was to ask about colleagues with whom I had worked, such questioning was mostly about their spending habits.

On completion of the Admin course I was posted to a Radar Station in Norfolk, a station that for some reason did not rate a Station Warrant Officer, but did rate a Flight Sergeant in charge of Discipline and Good Order, in this instance myself. The duties there were as I have already mentioned, rather monotonous and at times boring but I stuck with it for a little under 18 months and eventually, because of ensuing events decided to call it a day. One of my final duties before I left was to train a Guard of Honour for the AOC's (Air Officer Commanding) annual visit and inspection. Being now a qualified DI (Drill Instructor) I thought this was going to be routine, until that is I paraded the potential honour guard for the first time. By now the FN 7.62mm Self-Loading rifle was the standard firearm on issue and this is what the squad were issued with. My first question to them before starting on the routine, was, "how many of you have never previously drilled with this rifle?" The hands of almost every member of the squad shot up, so it was not going to be the piece of cake I thought it was after all. Every one of this squad was in the Radar trades, either operators, mechanics or fitters so would have had very little reason to have spent much time on the parade ground. I must say I was most pleasantly surprised with the cooperation I received and that I had the undivided attention of every single one of them at each training session. Maybe the fact that they knew that I was not a dyed-in-the-wool DI but a former tradesman had something to do with this, I don't know. Whatever the reason, I could not have asked for a better squad.

Came the day of the AOC's visit and my job was done, I was to take no further part in the ceremonies and retired to my office. I did meet the AOC briefly however when he paid a visit to the Sergeants' Mess during the lunch break, other than that I was kept out of sight. Later that day, after the AOC had long departed and returned to wherever he normally holed up, walking along the road en-route to my office the Station Commander, a Wing Commander, driving along the same road, stopped alongside me. Lowering his car window he handed me a copy of a teleprinted signal he had just received from the AOC. The signal contained the words, 'that was the best guard of honour I have seen during my time as AOC of the Group'. The station commander was obviously very pleased and was smiling all over his face, something I had not very often witnessed. This station commander was of a moralistic bent and I don't believe he was particularly happy to have me on his station because of my marital state. Furthermore, I don't think he thought that this ex-Special Operator Flight Sergeant turned DI and

General Duties Wallah could have made anything like a decent job of training a guard of honour. I was happy to have proved him wrong.

I took my discharge from the Royal Air Force on the day before my fortieth birthday and took my place in a world I had not known since I left it at the tender age of 16 years. By this time my partner had given birth to our daughter bringing the number in the household to five and I was still paying maintenance to my wife so this would have given the authorities more reason to get twitchy should I have remained in the service and in sigint in particular.

At first we were indeed having something of a struggle to make ends meet, both my partner and I were in low paid jobs but both actively looking to improve the situation. During my time in Australia I had taken an interest in stamp collecting and had the good fortune to find myself with a small but decent high value collection. This came about because one fellow employee through his habit of gambling heavily found himself in financial difficulty from time to time. Knowing of my hobby he offered to sell me some of his Falklands Isle stamp collection at, according to others more knowledgeable than I, a very good price. It was a number of stamps from this collection that came to my rescue in time of need. My financial situation was by no means desperate but some extra cash was needed to stay solvent so I sold two mint condition unused high value Queen Victoria stamps to a London dealer by post and never looked back. Sad that it had to be one person's misfortune, albeit through his gambling habit, that helped me in my time of need. Perhaps I should add here that this particular fellow was employed in a purely administrative capacity at DSB and had no access to classified material. Should it have been otherwise and his gambling habits were well known, he would certainly have been treated as a security risk and would not have lasted long in the job.

I eventually found employment with a large pharmaceutical company and after a couple of years in the job rose to a well-paid managerial position. My partner was also employed by the same company so although we did not own our house, we were comfortable, could afford a decent car and at least one holiday abroad per year. As part of my job I was responsible for the purchase of the cars for the use of the department's managers and field staff that numbered upwards of sixty. I was also charged with the disposal of these vehicles when they had attained high mileage that was, in the case of the representatives and their managers in the field usually less than two years. Prior to sending these used cars to auction or disposing of them otherwise I was able to use them for field visits and the like, arriving home in such a vehicle following a visit. These cars were, in the main, still smart looking vehicles, and in the case of those previously used by the managerial staff they may have been an up market model. This coupled with my holidays abroad and maybe a couple of slightly extended holiday week-end visits to my very good friend on the Isle of Skye no doubt had my neighbours thinking I had won the football pools. The national lottery was yet to be introduced.

So much of what my neighbours may have thought but I do suspect that in other quarters someone was thinking along different lines. And there was me thinking that I was being left alone to get on with my life. My suspicions that I was now, once again being 'looked at' were first aroused when one morning whilst living in Stockport, Greater Manchester. Prior to leaving the house on an errand and wanting to make a telephone call I discovered that my telephone was out of order. As I had used the phone a short while previous this 'fault' had obviously just occurred but needing to go out I decided I would report it when I had finished my business. However, driving around the corner I noticed what I presumed was a BT engineer at one of those large green junction box affairs. Ah! Thought I, I'll have a quick word. More than a word really but just a question, "are you sorting the problem out at No.31?" to my amazement, "yes" he replied looking somewhat flustered and surprised. I hadn't even reported the phone out of order at this time but here was someone fixing it, he was fixing it all right.

On another occasion, returning home from work one evening a neighbour told me that a well-dressed chap who had been parked outside the house for some time approached her and asked if she knew me. He told her he had known me in Berlin and brought the questioning around to such things as how long she had known me. This lady's description of the questioner did not ring any bells with me and he was never to reappear.

However, the most blatant attempt at surveillance reared its ugly head a good many years later. A short holiday at a nice rural guest house in Somerset was planned and all the arrangements were made on the phone. At the guest house we found ourselves in the company of about six or seven other couples. The male of one couple had 'copper' written all over him, not a problem there, even policemen and the like are entitled to holidays. This fellow soon engaged us in conversation and after a couple of days there asked if we would like to accompany him and his wife to a nearby pub that evening. I was not keen, not that I had anything against the couple but we had a small dog with us and as I explained to the fellow, I was not keen to leave her alone for too long in a place with which she was not familiar. It was left at that but a little later that day I took the dog out for a walk in the fields adjacent to the guest house. As I was returning but still had a fair way to go this fellow appeared, there was nowhere he could really be going except to the main road and as he approached he repeated his invitation to join him and his wife in a trip to a nearby pub, in fact he almost pleaded so I gave in and he agreed he would drive us all to the pub later.

The first shock on arrival at a very nice country pub was the welcome this chap received from the landlord. He was greeted like an old friend and first names were used, it was almost like he was a local whereas he had told me during chat at the meal table that he was from the other side of the country, St. Albans I think it was. Drinks were duly ordered but we were not to stay in the bar, we were steered into what is generally referred to as the lounge, a back room in fact, in which we were the only occupants. Early on the conversation came around to what we did and had previously done for a living; he said he was an engineer. Regarding my RAF service I gave the standard reply saying I was in Signals and eventually after more chit-chat he, to my surprise, brought the subject around to sigint mentioning a few stations he knew of that had been in operation during the war. I didn't give a lot of thought to that as many people who had lived adjacent to such places and apparently he had, would have done the same once they had learned of the purpose of such stations. What did get me thinking however was that whatever subject was under discussion he always managed to bring it around or back to what I had been doing and to sigint in general. Should I still have been in the RAF or had only a short time passed since leaving the service I may have thought it was an attempt to recruit me but as neither was the case I gave no credence to that. This couple departed the next day but I no longer remember if he had cut his holiday short or not. Regardless of that I still found it all rather strange. Readers may be forgiven for perhaps thinking I had become paranoid about such matters but to me the evidence was there.

Finally, I feel perhaps it is appropriate to reveal details of the final insult bestowed upon me whilst I was still a Spec Op and prior to the dramatic events of Douglas Britten's treachery. This alone could well have resulted in me requesting my discharge from the service but it did not. The reasons already given in Chapter 7 still hold true.

Shortly after arriving back at Digby in 1968 it was announced that the annual AOC's parade and inspection was soon to take place. Following this announcement I was informed by the SWO, Andy Fearny, a really nice guy, that as I was to receive my BEM from the AOC on this parade I would need a new 'Best Blue' uniform. He was of the opinion that the one I was currently wearing and that had been reclining in the bottom of kit bag for at least the last four years was not really fit for such an occasion. Oh dear, scruffy me. So it was off to the tailor's shop where I was duly measured and very soon issued with nice new uniform. Now nicely spruced up I was later to report to the station adjutant where I was asked for details of the local newspaper close to my home town in order that the appropriate notice of the event could be notified for publication. The notice was also to appear in the

Lincolnshire Echo.

The day prior to this event arrived and late that afternoon I was summoned to the Station Commander's office. The time to report that was conveyed to me seemed rather strange. It was certainly after 1700 hours when just about all the staff in the Station Headquarters had shut up shop and gone home or back to their accommodation. I entered SHQ via the front door, an entrance restricted to Officers only. I was supposed to use the 'tradesman's entrance' at the rear. Oh how the service reeked, and maybe still does, of class distinction. It was indeed quiet inside the building so I went straight to the Wing Commander's office, knocked and entered. Wing Co. was seated with another officer standing alongside him, and it all looked very ominous. I approached his desk and did the saluting bit, I was not of course asked to sit down, obviously whatever was about to happen was not going to take very long. The Wing Commander opened the proceedings by saying something to effect that I was not now to be presented with my 'gong' on the parade after all. He was of the opinion, he said, that the ceremony would be reported in the press one day and possibly shortly after because of my present marital state would appear in the media in something like the *News of the World*. Somewhat taken aback but secretly not giving a shit I had nothing to say. He then went on to say, "of course we could withhold the medal". Like hell he could, if he really intended to do that then I certainly would have had something to say. That medal was earned, not only by myself working sometimes eighteen hour days in S E Asia but by the support of my colleagues in the unit. This was a medal recommended by those who were of the opinion that I deserved it, was then further approved by the Prime Minister of the day himself and finally endorsed by no other than her most gracious Majesty Queen Elizabeth II. Now here was a minor cog in the hierarchy talking about withholding it. My thoughts were, withhold it, just bloody try and the media will certainly hear about it. I continued to hold my tongue waiting for further threats and was wondering if he was going to do the honours himself and pin the medal on my nice new uniform with me in it. Oh no, the final blow below the belt was yet to be delivered.

His next words being "collect your medal from the mail room on the way out".

The mail room had but one solitary occupant at that time, a young Senior Aircraftman who obviously knew why I was there. Without a word but looking somewhat embarrassed, the poor lad handed me a small package. That was it, ceremony of receiving one British Empire Medal concluded. I think I must be the only person entitled to wear that rose pink ribbon with the pearl grey stripes at its edges and through its centre that had been presented with it, still in its packaging, by a young airman.

I don't think for one moment that the reason I was given for this insulting and what was probably meant to be a degrading episode was the true one. It was more likely that the AOC, being briefed on the events to take place the next day and learning to whom he was expected to present a medal to and shake the hand of, decided he wanted no part of it. So many years have now passed since these events and since that experience at the guest house I don't recall anything further that that would give me cause to think that I may still be a 'suspect'. Now as I write, in my eighty-fifth year, happily retired in a quiet and beautiful part of mainland Europe, I have some wonderful memories of my time in the RAF. Such memories overshadow the shabby treatment received in my last couple of years service.

ABBREVIATIONS

AA Automobile Association

A&E Accident and Emergency

AOC Air Officer Commanding

AURI Angkatan Udara di Republic Indonesia. The Indonesian Air Force.

BAFVS British Armed Forces Vouchers.

BEM British Empire Medal

BMC British Motor Corporation.

BMH British Military Hospital

BRIXMIS The British Commander in Chiefs Mission to the Soviet Forces in Germany.

CO Commanding Officer

CTS Central Training School) GCHQs training school located at Bletchley Park)

DDR Deutsche Democratic Republic (the old East Germany)

DI Drill Instructor

DP Displaced Person or Refugee

DF Direction Finding

DSB Defence Signals Branch. Name later changed to DSD

DSD Defence Signals Directorate

ELINT Electronic Intelligence

EOKA Ethniki Organosis Kyprion Agoniston (Greek Cypriot Guerrilla Organisation)

EWS Emergency Water Supply

Flt.Lt Flight Lieutenant

FN Fabrique Nationale d'Herstal a leading arms manufacturer located in Belgium.

GCA Ground Control Approach

GCHQ Government Communications Headquarters

GDT Ground Defence Training

GS General Search

HF High Frequency

HFDF High Frequency Direction Finding

HMS Her Majesty's Ship

HMT Hired Military Transport

i/c In charge of

ICAO International Civil Aviation Organisation

ID Identity (usually some form of identity card or passport)

JAP J A Prestwich – Manufacturers of small petrol powered generators

JSSU Joint Service Signals Unit

MC/S Megacycles now more commonly mHz Megahertz

MET Meteorological

MOD Ministry of Defence

MT Motor Transport

NAAFI Navy Army And Air Force Institute

NATO North Atlantic Treaty Organisation

NCO Non-Commissioned Officer

NSA National Security Agency

NSFK Nationalsozialistisches Fliegerkorps Part of the Hitler Youth organisation

NSW New South Wales Australia

OC Officer Commanding

OR Other Rank

OTP One Time Pad

P&SS Provost and Security Services. An RAF Police Unit.

PDU Personnel Despatch Unit

POW Prisoner Of War

PPI Planned Position Indicator

PTI Physical Training Instructor

RAAF Royal Australian Air Force

RAF Royal Air Force

RAFVR Royal Air Force Voluntary Reserve

RCN Royal Canadian Navy

RDF Radio Direction Finding

RN Royal Navy

RNZAF Royal New Zealand Air Force

RO Radio Operator or Radio Officer

RPKAD Resimen Para Komando Angkatan Darat. An elite army parachute regiment.

RSGB Radio Society of Great Britain

R/T Radio Telephony

SAC Senior Aircraftman

SHQ Station Headquarters

SIB Special Investigation Branch

SIGINT Signals Intelligence

SIO Senior Intelligence Officer

SIS Secret Intelligence Service MI6

SU Signals Unit

SNCO Senior Non-commissioned Officer

SP Service Policeman (RAF Police)

1. SRO Station Routine Order

STOL Short Take Off and Landing

SU Signals Unit

SWO Station Warrant Officer

TA Traffic Analysis

TPT Tent Peg Toe

UHF Ultra High Frequency

USAF United States Air Force

VHF Very High Frequency

VoPo Volkspolizei, East German Police

WPM Words Per Minute

WRANS Women's Royal Australian Naval Service

WWI World War One

WWII World War Two

YMCA Young Men's Christian Association

NOTES

[ ] See GCHQ, A Signals Intelligence trailblazer, 1918-1964 (internet)

[2] NAAFI Navy, Army & Air Force Institute. A bar/canteen and shop for the Forces.

[3] Jankers. Armed Forces slang for the punishment of being confined to camp.

[4] The Royal Rifles of Canada Hong Kong War Diary 1st to 25th December 1941.

[5] Veteran Affairs Canada. 'Canadians in Hong Kong'

[6] Wikipedia HMS Amethyst (F116)
[7] Wikipedia HMS Amethyst (F116)
[8] Wikipedia Lei Yue Mun Park and Holiday Village.

[9] Padi, the Malay word for rice as it is growing in the field. Often spelt as Paddy.

[10] JAP. J.A. Prestwich, the manufactures of these engines.

[11] SROs a form of bulletin regularly posted on notice boards.

[2] Pongo, a mild derogatory term for any member of the British Army.

[3]Whilst two would be on watch, at weekends usually reduced to one on the daytime shift.
[14] SPYCATCHER: Peter Wright pub. Viking Penguin Inc. p86

[15] Internet: Scale Soaring UK, colours and markings of German gliders 1922-1945

[16] George Blake Super Spy. H. Montgomery Hyde. Futura

[17] The Springing of George Blake. Cassell & Co

[18] Source. The Irish Examiner 16 February 2012

[19] OTP. If used correctly possibly the most secure encryption system.

[20] BRIXMIS see *BRIXMIS by* Tony Geraghty published by Harper Collins

[21] The Villa, the Lake, The Meeting, Wannsee and the Final Solution - Mark Roseman - Penguin Books.

[22] Wikipedia Glienicke Bridge

[23] Avus. Automobil Verkehrs und Übungs Strasse - Automobile Traffic and Practice Road
[24] Wikipedia Hay New South Wales.

[25] This is a small blue card upon which is printed all the departments on the station, Medical Centre, Dental Centre, pay accounts, and many more. New arrivals must take this personally to these places where they will be 'logged in' and the form duly signed and dated. That way all that need to know are aware that one has arrived on the station.
[26] If possessing language skills was not a necessary part of ones normal trade, successful completion of a course of instruction and subsequent examination personnel would, as an incentive be awarded a bounty, I think at this time it was £120. .

[27] Atap. Although these native dwellings are often referred to as atap huts or houses, atap actually refers to the roof that is often of palm-leaf thatching.

[28] Desert Lilly. A large plastic funnel, also known to some as a Tun dish, inserted into a short length of heavy duty plastic or rubber tubing the end of which was buried in the ground in a mixture of soil or sand and stones with the funnel standing upright - a urinal.

[29] Hexamine Fuel Tablet; a tablet of solid fuel. These very efficient high energy smokeless tablets leave no ashes or liquid deposits. One must however use only outdoors where possible and be very careful not to breath in the toxic fumes.

[30] Electronic Intelligence. The gathering of intelligence by the interception of radar and weapons guidance systems to establish the capabilities of such systems.

[31] Humint, Human Intelligence; a spy in place on the ground.

[32] Source. Internet: Negeri Sembilan State Chinese Sufferance during Japanese Occupation. By Chinese assembly Hall of Negeri Sembilan State.

[33] Since 2002 this area has been a protected place but a number of dives have been controversially sanctioned.

[34]   2nd TAF Was formed during WWII and later went through a number of name changes reverting again to Second Tactical Air Force in late 1951 and being located, as it had for some years post war, in Germany.

[35] GRO Index Army Marriages (1881 -1955)
[36] Govt. White Paper Cmnd. 3856 November 1968. Report of the Security Commission

[37] Govt. White Paper Cmnd. 3856 November 1968. Report of the Security Commission.
[38] GRO Reg .290 vol 7 P.1814

ABOUT THE AUTHOR

Chris Boyd was born and brought up close to the city of Manchester in England later moving to and finishing his schooling in the beautiful mountainous countryside of North Wales. He enlisted in the Royal Air Force at the age of sixteen and initially trained as a Telegraphist. After a very short time he entered into the secret world of Signals Intelligence where he was employed, in various locations eavesdropping on the wireless communications of other nations. During this time he undertook language training and learnt German and Indonesian.

Upon leaving the RAF he was employed for thirteen years by a large pharmaceutical company in a number of positions before becoming the Manager of Administration Services. He took early retirement and went off around Europe in a camper van for four months. On return to the UK he became self employed providing security and support services for major international airlines. Following his final retirement he lived on the island of Cyprus for seven years, the Italian South Tyrol for a short time before moving to South West France where he now lives with his charming French partner.

CPSIA information can be obtained
at www.ICGtesting.com
Printed in the USA
LVOW04s1948151116
513060LV00010B/1324/P